CELTIC
QUEST

CELTIC QUEST

A Healing Journey
for Irish Catholics

TIMOTHY J. JOYCE

ORBIS BOOKS

Maryknoll, New York 10545

Second Printing, February 2001

The Catholic Foreign Mission Society of America (Maryknoll) recruits and trains people for overseas missionary service. Through Orbis Books, Maryknoll aims to foster the international dialogue that is essential to mission. The books published, however, reflect the opinions of their authors and are not meant to represent the official position of the society.

To obtain more information about Maryknoll and Orbis Books, please visit our website at www.maryknoll.org.

Manufactured in the United States of America

Library of Congress Cataloging-in-Publication Data

Joyce, Timothy J.
    Celtic quest : a healing journey for Irish Catholics / Timothy J. Joyce
      p. cm.
    Includes bibliographical references (p.).
    ISBN 1-57075-334-2 (pbk.)
    1. Irish American Catholics – Religious life. 2. Spiritual life – Celtic Church. I. Title

BX1407.I7 .J69 2000
282′.73′0899162 – dc21

                          00-037478

Contents

Introduction

IN 1998 I published a book, *Celtic Christianity: A Sacred Tradition, A Vision of Hope,* that explored the world of the first-millennium Celtic Christian Church, its people and particular gifts.[1] Among other things, I wanted to show how the early Christian Celts embraced a particular spiritual worldview that eventually succumbed to the style of Irish Catholicism that is much more familiar to contemporary Catholicism both in Ireland and in America. I attempted to show that an understanding of this earlier Christian spirituality could be a source of renewal, and prove to be life-enriching to Christians today. I looked at how the Celtic saints, such as Patrick, Bridget, and Columcille, are fellow travelers on our spiritual journey today. I also looked at how Celtic spirituality, so rooted in the land and in nature, appeals to those of us who are sensitive to the environment and who are concerned about the current ecological crisis of our planet earth. I also reflected on how Celtic spirituality helps us in our appreciation of our human relationships, accepting the particular giftedness of both women and men, and building on our close connectedness to our ancestors. And I looked at how the richness of a poetic, imaginative, and holistic spirituality creates an entirely other dimension in contrast to an exclusively cerebral type of religion that only knows rules, laws, and doctrines.

The reflection on Celtic Christianity was, of course, the reflection on my own spiritual journey. In sharing this personal spiritual journey I have been delighted to find that many others identify with and corroborate so much of what I have written. My own story, with its fascination with things Celtic, began over twenty years ago. A number of circumstances led me to start searching for an understanding of Celtic history and for what I began to comprehend as the Celtic vision or a particular Celtic way of seeing reality, and how it affected spirituality. Initially, I probably was fascinated because I am an Irish American and I wanted to understand my own background and that of my ancestors. But I uncovered much more than I could ever have imagined. I began to see that the Celtic vision of the world, of God, of the church, and of the meaning of life had a particularly imaginative and holistic way of expressing itself. I discovered it to be extremely appealing and saw that it could be a tremendous help for my own spiritual life and for other people today on their spiritual journey.

My exploration into the Celtic world soon assumed a life of its own. Looking back, my whole involvement must have been guided by the Holy Spirit, whom some, in the Celtic tradition, have called the Wild Goose. One thing after another started happening. In 1994 I offered my first workshop in Celtic spirituality. I was still exploring various aspects of the topic then and I could offer only some very tentative material. But the Wild Goose helped me out. One of the participants at that first workshop was Mairead Loughnane Doherty, an Irish-born Celtic harpist and a very articulate and spiritual person. Wishing to make a Lenten retreat and finding the weekend of her choice fully booked, Mairead registered for the Celtic spirituality weekend instead. I asked her to join me in presenting future workshops and retreats and thus began a partnership that has been very enriching for both of us. Since then we have been doing four or five programs a year. Working together as man and woman, and sharing our different perspectives, we have together grown in our understanding and appreciation of the Celtic vision. Mairead has helped me refine many of the ideas that I put forward in this book.

The Holy Spirit was again active and busy when one of our retreatants asked me to put some of the workshop and retreat in print. He was Bob Gormley, at that time the executive director of the Catholic publishing house of Orbis Books, and this led to the publication of my first book. Soon after that I was asked by another publisher to write a book on Saint Patrick as part of a series on retreats with various saints and teachers.[2] I did not seek these tasks, but I do believe I was being directed by the Wild Goose to bring this spirituality to others. There is an obvious need and hunger for the Celtic vision.

The reactions to the workshops and the books have been most interesting, and often quite surprising. As I began to share this message in other talks and conferences as well as in the weekend programs, I became aware that I was touching something already deeply ingrained in or intuited by the listeners. It only needed someone to put words on the experience. People can often identify the Celtic story through their own life and story, their families, their backgrounds, and certain familiar behaviors they have observed but not always understood. A second surprise was that the message was often a catalyst of healing, freedom, liberation, and eventual reconciliation for many readers and audiences. One participant, Joan, wrote directly, "Though I've felt an exile my whole adult life, you have given me a glimpse of home." Another, Tom, said to me, "It has restored my sense of good self-esteem." We Catholics, Irish American Catholics in particular (though I also include Irish Canadians and Irish Australians in this view), have been heirs to a particular history that has left its residue of scars in the feelings, complexes, and sometimes distorted way of seeing things. Anger, frustration, guilt, and an ignorance or denial of what brought these on have all been part of the story. This is not to say that other ethnic groups, whether Catholic or otherwise, don't share these same, or similar, feelings, issues, problems, and views. There is a relationship of circumstances that has affected all of us who were influenced by the particular way the Catholic Church developed in the nineteenth-century expansion in the New World, and many who are not of Irish background also resonate with this story. We Irish Americans are scarred just as all groups are. It is by coming to know our story that we can discover a larger point of reference from which to look at our own lives. This is not a matter of facts and analysis but of becoming aware of something bigger than ourselves. We can stop blaming ourselves, our parents, our teachers, or the church and take responsibility for our own lives when we understand how we have gotten to where we are. We can end our adversarial relationship with the English, with Protestants (if we are Catholics, or vice versa), or with those more successful than we are, and learn to live in the present.

In these pages, then, we will look at the story of Irish American Catholicism, with its distinctive characteristics and idiosyncrasies. I will share some of the insights that have come to me in this work of uncovering Celtic Christianity, including the insights of those people who have shared with me the struggles and the stumbling steps of their own spiritual journeys. I hope that many more, in reading these pages and reflecting on their own lives in the light of our common story, will be enlightened to move on to a path of creative, wholesome living, and be helped to find a healthier and more fruitful Christian life.

Chapter One

American Catholics and Their Journey

W HEN I FIRST BEGAN to speak and write about my view and understanding of Irish American Catholic spirituality and its relation to Celtic Christianity, I found that not all reactions were positive nor was my message always understood. An abridged version of one of my talks appeared in a newsletter dedicated to sharing information about Celtic spirituality.[3] Here are excerpts from one person's response to that article.

> The last newsletter contained a feature cover article written by you about Irish Catholicism. I did not enjoy your article. In fact, to be quite frank, I resented some of your insinuations such as: 1. The word "catholic" used to refer to Roman Catholics only. I am a former Roman Catholic. I matured into a practicing catholic once I entered the Episcopal Church. 2. The implication that American Catholicism revolves around the Irish contribution only, which was heavily influenced by Celtic impartiality. I am a former Roman Catholic. Why? Because the Irish refused my Grandparents a seat in THEIR Roman Catholic Church. Therefore the Italians built their own and distanced themselves from the Irish hierarchy by calling in priests from Italy to minister to them. 3. If you really look at Celtic spirituality, and if the

Irish really endorse it, which they should because it is more familiar to them, then the Irish too would distance themselves from the Roman Catholic Church and become catholic in the process themselves. Sorry, but you hit one of my sore nerves. It has taken me years to get over the abuse that I experienced in the Roman Church. Anamchairde seems to be headed in the same direction of maudlin expressions of Irish Roman Catholicism.

This letter expresses a view from outside the Irish American community. I don't believe it is particularly unusual. An Italian American priest speaks of his experience as a student at Boston College, the Jesuit institution founded in the 1800s expressly for Irish American Catholic boys. Attending this institution in the 1960s, this priest friend of mine felt that, as an Italian, he was a distinct minority, and sometimes a persecuted one at that. A French American Catholic who attended one of our workshops described his feelings of being an outsider in his parish, especially on Saint Patrick's Day. He also admitted, however, that hearing the Irish story helped him to see that the Irish community was not such a strong and trouble-free group as he had perceived it to be. This reflection also led him to look at his own roots and how his own understanding of Catholicism was influenced by both Irish and French Canadian history. Therefore, at the outset, it is important to comprehend how the Irish American experience touched many other ethnic groups. It should be remembered that the Catholic Church, as established in the United States in the nineteenth century, was largely an immigrant church composed of many national and ethnic groups, mostly from Europe. The Irish model of the church in North America, however, overshadowed all other European experiences, so that no matter what country you came from in Europe, you would find the local parish reflecting Irish ways. Already we can see our topic in a wider context, affecting all Catholics in the New World and, because of the large waves of Catholic immigrants, impacting the entire fabric of American society. The reality of an Irish church being implanted in a new world and becoming the dominant model of church was played out in similar ways in English-speaking Canada and Australia. I will come back to this point later.

The letter quoted at the beginning of this chapter also portrays how some, as they become disillusioned with the aftermath of the Irish influence on the Catholic Church, look elsewhere for a spiritual home. They might abandon all religious adherence and drift off into a completely secular way of living within the American culture and, often, unconsciously accept the civil religion of American culture as a substitute. Alternatively, they may become aware of their spiritual roots and realize that they still feel a spiritual longing. As they get in touch with the feelings and confusing thoughts that usually accompany this longing, there is often a lot of anger. The inadequate Christian education that was given in the early twentieth century often resulted in a narrow understanding of life, of Christ and the gospel, of ways to live the Christian message in family and society. The realization that guilt has been such a large part of their upbringing can also produce anger. People feel that they have been cajoled into pleasing God and family, into being good and law-abiding practitioners of the faith, because of the fear of hell and/or the fear of priests, nuns, and parents. This type of guilt is not the kind of appropriate guilt that reflects a sense of responsibility after doing something that is evil or hurtful. It is, rather, a guilt that is shameful and tends to make one feel personally evil, in contrast to recognizing one's evil actions. For many people, the awareness of these feelings increases the level of their anger.

Restlessness and Rebellion

I am constantly amazed, but no longer surprised, to find Catholics, nonpracticing Catholics, or former Catholics (however they describe themselves) in so many other spiritual settings these days. I have attended, for instance, some meetings of Alcoholics Anonymous and other similar "program" meetings. There I have encountered hurt and humbled people who, although they have made a mess of their lives, have found the dignity and honesty as graced human beings to pick up the pieces and move on. There are a lot of Catholics, and Catholics of Irish descent in particular, in such gatherings. You can get quite an earful of their angry feelings that are a reaction to the guilt supposedly inflicted on them by parents or priests. These men and women often become very spiritual people while at the same time rejecting any kind of religion other than their Twelve Step program. Like many others in today's society, they separate spirituality from religion and do not see the need for belonging to any church community.

On the other hand, many Catholics hunger for a religious home that is both spiritual and institutional. This often seems to be the case for those who are Irish born or Irish American. Religion has always been part of the Irish cultural scene, and it has been difficult to separate religion from the very identity of the Irish. Though this may be changing with the increasing secularization in Ireland, a popular saying states, "You can always take an Irishman out of the church but you can't take the church out of an Irishman." This doesn't apply only to simple and uneducated people. Brian Moore is an interesting person to consider in this regard. Moore, who died in early 1999, was an outstanding writer of fiction. Born in Northern Ireland, he spent much of his life in Canada, Australia, and the United States. His novels[4] all treat issues of the spiritual search and the relationship of religion and life.

Themes of guilt, sin, and religion always preoccupied him. At the same time, he claimed that he was never convinced of the value of religion. He said he did not even believe in God. But he would add, "I am certainly fascinated by those who do." Such a sentiment seems to be part of the Irish psyche.

So it is not surprising to find Catholics or former Catholics or "recovering Catholics" (as some like to call themselves) involved in many other religious traditions. They are dissatisfied with the church, often angry with it, or they do not recognize it as a place to find spiritual guidance. As one man, Leo, put it to me, the church is not offering reasonable answers to his questions and only seems to want to control certain areas of his life, such as sexuality. Then there is my friend, Ed, reared as a Catholic, who became an Episcopalian and is now seriously practicing Zen Buddhism. He, and many others of Irish Catholic roots, attend Buddhist retreats and go to Buddhist centers to learn from this tradition.[5] Still other Catholics seek a spiritual home in the Hindu tradition. Nearby our monastery, here in Massachusetts, we have the Vedanta Center, a Hindu-style ashram. Though I am unaware of its present composition, I know that many former Catholics have composed part of its community in years past. Similarly, Bede Griffiths, an English Benedictine monk who spent the last forty years of his life in India adapting Christian monasticism to the Hindu model in an ashram, also attracted many American and European Catholics seeking a deeper spiritual life.

A number of Catholics I know are being drawn into the New Age movement. They say that they find many positive things there and that the movement provides ways to connect to the earth and to a sense of an imminent God. I find it insufficient myself inasmuch as it remains a loose movement and usually bypasses any sense of long-term commitment to community, as well as sacrifice and service, though I respect the spiritual awakening it provides for a number of people. Then there is Paul, who came from a very conservative Irish Catholic family and who became a charismatic Christian. Now he has embraced Native American spirituality — sweat lodges, vision quests, peace pipes, and so forth. He is drawn to this expression of spirituality, an expression that he did not find in his Christian background, but one that is based on oneness with the earth and all creation. This is a serious commitment for him, and in response to its social justice dimension, he helps to gather supplies and clothing for poor Native American children on reservations. Yes, many Catholics have found these traditions very helpful in finding a spiritual path for themselves. I am saddened, however, to discover that many dissatisfied Catholics are searching along many diverse paths but have no realization that there is a mystical tradition within their own religious background.

Another group that finds itself dissatisfied with its Catholic background is women, and an increasing number of men too, who find the patriarchal church oppressive and unaccepting of their own experience and the feminine dimension of life. Those who come to believe that Christianity is intrinsically male in its orientation and in its control of power, and that all the principal symbols of God are male, often seek a different religious expression or another Christian church where women are accepted more readily, where their gifts are acknowledged, where their voices are heard, and where they are encouraged to take part in the decision making of the church.

A Yearning for the Old and the New

Perhaps the great interest in Celtic spirituality can be best understood in the context of this emerging interest in so many diverse spiritual traditions. This older Celtic expression of the Christian church has a lot with which to commend itself to spiritual searchers today. One major reason for its attractiveness may be that it predates a lot of the divisions in the Christian world that have torn Christians apart.

During the second millennium the development of cities and nations resulted in great advances in human achievement and progress. Music, art, literature, medicine, and universal education flourished. Science and technology brought a human standard of living that could not have been envisioned during the first thousand years of the Christian era. Human slavery was finally rejected throughout most of the planet. Unfortunately, this was also a millennium of violence and large-scale warfare. Greed and domination by colonialist empires marked this time. While human rights and the rights of individual races and ethnic groups have become more important, the larger human community has begun to suffer because of the extreme demand of individual rights. Something has been lost. The ecological movement has raised our awareness that we have become estranged from nature and have lost our connection to the earth. The feminist revolution has shown us how the female and the feminine part of creation have been subordinated and often subjugated by a patriarchal culture.

The church had formerly been a central reality in the lives of people in the early and medieval times of Christianity. So much of social, economic, and cultural life revolved around one's participation in the church, which was the dominant voice in society. But the church has lost much of its significance in modern times. Even more strikingly, the inner life of the Christian church has suffered from a number of developments in the second thousand years of its existence. I am not trying to suggest here that all was well and ideal in the first millennium. There were plenty of problems, and I do not advocate going back to a former age. Rather, the advances that have been made should be appropriated without ignoring the negative aspects. Some restoration of first-millennium perspectives, however, could help to balance us again. For instance, we will soon observe the millennial anniversary of the split of the Eastern and Western Christian church in 1054. That was a tragedy of great proportions that has resulted in a substantial loss to the West. The church in western Europe, and later in America, developed as very cerebral, practical, legal, moralistic, and authoritarian. The mystical and holistic vision of the East, with its stress on contemplation, has been neglected. In the Western stress on good moral living, there has been an excessive emphasis on sin and guilt, while the East has emphasized the divine call to divinization in the life of the Trinity. Part of the allure of Celtic Christianity is its connectedness with the tradition of the East in a much more intensive way than can be found in the rest of the Western church.

In the sixteenth century the Christian church of the West was further torn apart in the cataclysm of the Protestant Reformation. While bringing much needed reform and many positive new expressions of the Christian community, it also brought much tragedy and loss. The body of Christ was torn apart and to this day lives in a divided and often conflictual state. Persecution by one division of Christianity against the other has been part of the violent and warring history of modern times. Nowhere is this sadder than in the Celtic countries. Once sharing a common vision, these countries were pitted against each other as they embraced variants of the Christian church — Catholic Ireland, Anglican England, Presbyterian Scotland, Methodist Wales. The tragedy has reached its apogee in the relentless violence that has characterized the Republican (Catholic) versus Unionist (Protestant) in the nationalistic conflict and division of Northern Ireland.

As Americans, we may consider the Reformation and its aftermath with an attitude of nonchalance. Since religion for Americans is often a matter of subjective opinion and personal taste, many do not see the division of Christians as especially problematic. In this study of Celtic Christianity, my working together with members of other Christian churches has raised my awareness of what a tragedy this splintering has been and remains for us. By accentuating that which distinguishes us and makes us different from other Christians, we have often been deprived of knowing, and being enriched by, the deeper, common Christian tradition, with its story of Christ, the Trinity, the gospel, contemplative prayer, and genuine service to the human family, even if these are expressed in a diversity of ways.

Another historical factor that had negative repercussions on Christian spirituality was the Enlightenment of the eighteenth century. This movement separated the mind from the spirit and led to all sorts of dualisms, eventually relegating religion and spirituality to the private domain. It also abetted the scientific mentality that reduces knowledge to that which can be proved factually by mathematical and biological tools. We have been driven further and further along the trail to an isolated, individualistic state of mind that leaves people anxious and spiritually gasping for air. We know we have lost something. We yearn for a more connected kind of understanding of our relationship to God, people, and the cosmos.

Responses from the Christian Tradition

Neglected parts of our Christian tradition are reemerging in our day. The mystical and prophetic elements of Christianity, as well as a more intellectual approach to religion, are reappearing to balance the institutionalized weight of the recent centuries. There are a number of such movements and traditions. It comes as a surprise to many people that the church has not been as monolithic in its history as they have been led to believe. There have been many traditions and many spiritualities. It seems that some of the older ones are promising to be valuable for our own day.

Let me make a small digression for the purpose of clarification. I am not saying that all Catholics are ardently seeking to deepen their spiritual lives. There are many Catholics who have come through the past forty years with little change in their religious lives. They feel that the church, as institution, continues to support them in their lives. For some of them, change is not sought after inasmuch as they wish to remain rooted in the religious practices of their youth. A minority of people is even determined to restore the pre–Vatican II Catholic Church, with its certainties and securities. A third group, and it may be a large group at that, are simply apathetic. Religion has been part of their lives, but they can take it or leave it. Some, indeed, continue to attend church regularly but with no deep convictions. And some have left it without a whimper. For these, there is no anger, no sense of loss, no turning to look elsewhere, but simply the abandonment of their childhood faith and religion. The secular culture has filled the void for them. They would never be reading a book like this one!

With that caveat, we turn back to those who do feel anger or the need to search. These are the ones for whom an institutional-church experience is no longer enough. One reason for this dissatisfaction is a much better and more intelligent understanding of the faith. Many, many laymen and laywomen have studied theology, have read serious books or periodicals, and have attended retreats and workshops. A definite conversion experience may have occurred for those who have been involved in the charismatic renewal movement, or who have lived a Cursillo weekend or a similar in-depth experience. A search for a deeper, more regular prayer life and some community support usually follow these kinds of experiences.

While remaining more or less in the mainstream of parish life, groups of Catholics and other Christians have turned to regular meditation, seeking a contemplative prayer life. The Centering Prayer advocated by the Cistercian monks William Meninger, Basil Pennington, and Thomas Keating has drawn many adherents. Others have formed meditation groups based on John Main's mantric prayer in the tradition of the fourth-century monastic writer John Cassian.[6] Benedictine spirituality has come back into the consciousness of many laypeople who find the sixth-century Rule of Saint Benedict a valid guide for prayer and community in the modern world.[7] Numerous lay people have written commentaries on the Rule from a lay point of view.[8]

Medieval mystics such as Meister Eckhart, Hildegard of Bingen, and Julian of Norwich speak to many moderns. Bespeaking an ancient wisdom, they offer a mystical and unified vision of reality in which God is all in all and immanently present in all. Somewhat parallel to this insight is the work of many contemporary feminist writers who remind us of the value of human experience, connectedness to the earth and people, and the particular neglected values of the feminine. Recovery of this ancient wisdom provides a much needed balance in theology and spirituality for many in today's world.

Celtic Spirituality as a Response to the Search

Along with all these traditions and movements, Celtic spirituality is thus one of many traditions that are speaking to modern Catholic seekers. It has an advantage of being an older way of life that was actually lived in the church for centuries. It is not an ideology but a way of seeing things that has been concretized in various practices. It is part of our Western, Christian tradition. And, of course, it is a particularly good opening for Irish Americans and others who are trying to adjust the tradition they have learned to their yearning for something more. In the pages ahead we will look at the Celtic tradition. But in order to find the openness and perhaps the freedom and healing to do so, we will also consider the more recent tradition of Irish Catholic spirituality and the manner in which it has affected so many of us. We will thus attempt to gain a clearer awareness of where we are at the present moment.

This chapter has laid the groundwork for a comprehension of the situation in which we find ourselves and has opened the door to the possibility of another way to comprehend and live our Christian faith today. It has intimated that an acknowledgment of our dissatisfactions may have to be the first step in reimaging such a faith experience. I began with a quotation from a letter that expressed such dissatisfaction, and even anger. Now I would like to share my response to that letter.

> Thank you for your letter, Lou. I really do appreciate your taking the time to respond, though I realize it must have meant feeling some old pain. I apologize if I fed into an old wound. That article you read was an abbreviated version which, in turn, was a précis of a still longer talk. It seems the wrong message was conveyed. I do not really disagree with your position. In fact, I was trying to say that the nineteenth-century expression of Roman Catholicism that was brought to this country and made the basis of all the church (whether you were Irish, Italian, Polish, etc.) was his-

torically determined by very specific circumstances that need to be understood in context. But I was also calling for the need to get in touch with a much healthier, more ancient form of the Celtic tradition. It has been my experience that a lot of healing and liberation takes place in many people when they let go of what they now see as a very poor and inadequate spirituality. What I am seeking is a healing of anger, shame, and guilt for both individuals and the churches as a whole. I look for a better relationship with God, the earth, and each other in love and respect. Of course, I hope that happens in the Roman Catholic Church too, but if it takes you elsewhere, that is the work of the Spirit as well. Thank you again for taking the time to write. I ask the blessing of the holy Three-in-One God to encompass you in love and guide you on your own spiritual journey. May I ask you to say a prayer for me too?

I had to respond to this letter, for I understood why he needed to get those feelings out and I felt that he needed to know that he was heard. I was unsure whether he would accept what I offered to him. It seems that it did help him to let go of some of his anger, for I received the following reply.

Thanks for your response, which was very well composed in contrast to my "flying off the handle." For this I apologize, and I realize that there is ground for us to meet as brothers in Christ, once we get over the neuroses that have been given to us. Yes, I did say a prayer for you and continue to present your name before the Lord. I wish you success in your work and I hope that we can meet one day to revel in the compassion of Christ and to share his Eucharist together.

Chapter Two

The Faith of
Our Irish Ancestors

I WISH I HAD KNOWN my Irish grandparents. It is regrettable that they both died before I was born. I hope that the old Celtic belief that one has the spirit of one's grandparents (it skips over the intermediate generation) is true. I am named after both my grandfathers, and that has become significant for me as I grow older. But I do believe they are still with me, imparting their blessing to my own journey.

My mother used to tell a wonderful story about Grandma Joyce. It seems that she missed Mass one Sunday and then told this to a priest in confession. When the priest asked her if there was any reason for the lapse, she replied that it was none of his business. The truth was that she had mislaid her dentures when she was doing the wash and only later found that she had left them in the clothespin bag as she was hanging out the wash! The still deeper truth, for me, is that she exemplified something deep in the Irish Catholic psyche. She was attentive to her religious duties and took them seriously in a God-fearing fashion. But she didn't lose her human, independent spirit or her sense of humor. I am not sure that the next generation did as well in those areas. Perhaps this has been because the Irish sense of poetry and mysticism lost some of its central importance in its translation into the more literal and technological Anglo-Saxon world of North America.

Nineteenth-Century Irish Devotionalism

My Irish grandparents emigrated as young adults from Ireland around 1870. They had grown up in a church that had, in many ways, moved away from its traditional spirituality. It was a church rich in devotional practices — rosaries, novenas, missions, prayer cards, and spiritual nosegays. The sources of these prayers and practices, most of which were new to the Irish, were rooted in the restored Catholic Church in Victorian England and in the continental church in France, Belgium, and Italy. Some of these were in continuity with the old Celtic forms of piety that had been expressed in the Irish language. Thus, the new Devotion to the Sacred Heart, which became so popular with the Irish, appealed to them because they were an oppressed people who identified strongly with the passion and suffering of Christ as a loving savior, and with Mary, his sorrowful mother.

Other practices were completely new, particularly those that were now to be celebrated in the church as distinct from the home-centered practices of much of prefamine Ireland. Among these new devotions were the Benediction of the Blessed Sacrament, the Stations of the Cross, the communal praying of the rosary, and multiple novenas, to name a few examples. No longer were Mass and the sacraments celebrated in the home. The "Stations" in prefamine Ireland referred to the priest celebrating Mass in a particular neighborhood in a home. It is helpful to recall that most of the churches we see in Ireland today were built in the latter part of the nineteenth century. Of the old order, only the wake seemed to continue within the home context, and "Irish wakes" took on a particular mode of popular piety, as well as being great social occasions.

One weakness of this new postfamine church was a passivity in the face of authority and also in worship and the sacraments. The Mass was something the priest did for silent observers. This trend had been developing everywhere as people had lost contact with the Latin language in which the Mass was said. But, for the Irish, there was the additional circumstance of the secret, and therefore silent, Masses of the penal times. The Scriptures were not part of this spirituality, except as a book to reverence and to use to record family sacramental celebrations. In the past the Scriptures had been kept alive for the people in the many monastic centers that fed them. After the suppression of monasteries following the Reformation, they had neither this influence nor even the means to purchase books such as the Bible for themselves. And, as was the case in Europe at the time, there was little, if any, education in personal and contemplative prayer.

A strong allegiance to the pope was also part of this spirituality. Ever since the English moved into Ireland in the twelfth century, allegiance to the Bishop of Rome was important to the Irish as being the seat of the real authority over them and often a protection and aid against their colonial masters. Following the declaration of papal infallibility at the First Vatican Council in 1870, this greater loyalty and devotion to the pope was also part of a worldwide Catholic piety, and this only strengthened such a movement in Ireland. There the reverence for the papacy as well as the new forms of piety and devotion were strongly promulgated by Paul Cullen, archbishop of Dublin from 1852 to 1878. Paul Cullen had been rector of the Irish College in Rome and loved everything Roman. When he returned to Ireland from Rome, he preferred to speak Italian rather than Irish or English. He wanted the Irish church to be the most exemplary model of the Roman church. And this dream of his became a reality.

Church life was built on the centrality of the priest. The ordained priest became the focus of the parish and the unofficial leader of a village. During the penal times and the famine the priests had been close to the Irish in their suffering and loss. They were often the first to lose their lives. Priests had shown their love and devotion to the people, and in return the people respected and loved them. At first this was a good thing, for this new church was being built in a time of devastation. Eight hundred years of colonial domination, the decimation by events such as a plague in the fourteenth century and other similar experiences encountered by the entire medieval church had led to a dour, guilt-laden spirituality, one that stressed the need to make amends for sin. In the worldview that prevailed, the priest was important as a sign and instrument of God's forgiveness and reconciliation, the one who assured believers and penitents of the promise of salvation in a better world to come.

Roots of This New Church in the Past

By the nineteenth century the Irish probably had a more negative sense of humanity than many other peoples of Europe. The Reformation in the sixteenth century had led to an intensification of the division between Irish and English through the persecutions enacted by Queen Elizabeth I (1533–1603), who was determined to wipe out the Celtic culture and way of life. Things became even worse with the martyrdom suffered by the people under Oliver Cromwell (1599–1658). Many of the Irish were uprooted from the land and forced to move to the poorer areas of the west. This might not seem a major upheaval to us moderns who are always moving and on the go. But the Irish found their very identity in their connection with the land. It gave them meaning and security. Now they became a displaced people. This was followed, in turn, by the eighteenth-century penal laws, which deprived Catholics of such elemental rights as education, voting, and holding public office, and often imposed fines, imprisonment, or death. Catholics were required to take a public oath repudiating the pope, the real presence of Christ in the Eucharist, and other Catholic doctrines. Priests were rounded up and placed in concentration-camp-like enclaves on remote islands. Many were even killed by hanging. Families were broken up as thousands were sent into exile, some as indentured servants, or some as slaves to the West Indies and to American plantations. All of this was capped by the calamitous event of the Great Famine (1845–50). By the middle of the nineteenth century the Irish Catholic population, still the great majority of the island, was traumatized. The family was torn apart, men turned to drink, and women, who had been left to be the lone protectors and providers of children and family, often became hardened in the process. It must be understood that there were not only practical, physical effects from all of this tragedy but spiritual and emotional ones as well.

The Postfamine Irish Church

The late-nineteenth-century church thus moved into a tremendous vacuum. Catholic emancipation in Ireland had taken place in 1829. Now the bishops began to use their authority to bring significant improvement to the people with new church buildings and religious practices, schools and hospitals, social services and family support. It also promoted a new, narrower morality with an emphasis on sexual sins. The Irish had always had a strong ascetical bent and the old Celtic monks were known for their severe penances. Much of this was now focused more on atonement for sexual failings. The fostering and development of the Irish Catholic identity also meant a strong rejection of Protestants that often developed into anti-Protestantism and a self-righteous, intolerant form of Catholicism. The Irish sense of self could be expressed in the proclamation "I am Irish. I am not English. I am not Protestant."

All of this was, no doubt, a mixed bag of good and bad. The positive aspect can certainly be seen in the honor and dignity brought by the church to Irish Catholics. The building of a strong character and the teaching of solid moral principles was part of the religious training of the day. Discipline and self-control became important tools, useful in applying oneself to society's challenges. There was a sense of idealism that drew many to religious vocations and to the service and care of others. The new church did provide many practical benefits. But the spirituality was not always so positive. The image of God that motivated good and upright living was the image of a remote and judgmental God. One grew up with a fear of this God. To be sure, Mary and the saints were close, but God was not. Preached missions accentuated the fear of hell as a punishment for sins, particularly sexual sins of any kind, and the need for confession and penance to avoid hell. This certainly helped to establish a pervasive sense of guilt in people's lives and a sense of quiet passivity. The words *Irish* and *Catholic* were synonymous and interchangeable in many people's minds for years to come. For almost a hundred years the Irish Catholic Church remained a strong, practicing institution that did much good. It produced thousands of priests and nuns, more than enough for Ireland, and many went off as missionaries to different parts of the world.

A feeling of superiority and the sense that Ireland was *the* Catholic country also flourished in this setting. All of this came to a peak under John Charles McQuaid, the authoritarian and antiecumenical archbishop of Dublin in the years 1940–71.[9] McQuaid heavily influenced Eamon De Valera as head of government, and he was instrumental in prescribing the special status of the Catholic Church in the Irish Constitution adopted in 1937, even though his own preference for a Catholic theocratic state was not completely followed. There is no doubt that, as archbishop of Dublin during the war years and succeeding decades, he did a lot of good in the areas of education and public welfare. But he believed the rights of the one true Catholic Church had to be upheld, and he saw Protestants, Jews, Freemasons, and Communists as impinging on these rights. The Second Vatican Council, in its new openness to the world and other religions, was a terrible blow to his authority and views. Upon returning from Rome at the conclusion of the Second Vatican Council in 1965, he was met by reporters at the airport. He is said to have declared that much good had been done at the council but that it really wasn't needed in Ireland. One American priest told me that, when visiting Dublin in the 1960s, he was walking down the street when a car pulled up, and a priest emerged and told him that it was proper for priests to wear hats in public. It turned out to be Archbishop McQuaid himself! He had been determined to reform the Catholic Church in Ireland, beginning with the clergy.

The church thus became more and more authoritarian, continuing the trend set in the nineteenth century. William Butler Yeats (1864–1939), an Anglo-Irish Protestant, had attempted to find again the ancient Celtic culture and mythology for modern Ireland. One of his reasons for doing so was his perception of the Roman Catholic Church as narrow and anti-intellectual. Years later, another Irish writer, this one a Catholic himself, James Joyce, went into a self-imposed exile from Ireland, weary of the censorship and clerical smallness he found there. The ways of priests had all begun in a well-intentioned commitment to help the poor and the devastated Irish people. In many communities, the priest had been the only educated man, the only one who could read and write. He became indispensable for aiding his parishioners to get assistance in work and education, for reading letters from relatives in America and helping them to respond to them, and helping them in many other practical ways. Soon, however, he was telling them how to vote, how to think, how to be that perfect Irish Catholic in word and deed. Censorship became a common practice, a way to protect the poor people from being misled. Religious education was limited to a rote catechism approach to faith. When the structures of society and church are all secure and firm, this system might seem to work well. Many an Irish man and woman lived a firm and deep faith and were very loyal to their church. We see now, however, that when societal structures began to shift, the inner life was not firm enough to hold together for a large number of Catholics.

I have found the Irish Redemptorist priest John J. Ó Ríordáin very helpful in his excellent study *Irish Catholic Spirituality, Celtic and Roman.*[10] He provides the following insight into the new Irish Catholic Church of postfamine times.

> The Catholic philosopher and spiritual writer, Baron Friedrich von Hügel (1852–1925), distinguishes three elements in church life: the mystical, the intellectual and the institutional. If any one of these becomes dominant, if all three are not held in dynamic balance, each complementing and nourishing the others, the overall wellbeing suffers. In nineteenth-century Ireland the institutional element needed building up, but in the process the native Irish mystical element suffered serious eclipse and the intellectual element was not allowed room to develop freely. Many tensions in late twentieth-century Irish Catholicism are rooted in this imbalance.... [11]

I have found it helpful to review this recent history of Irish Catholicism, and readers may want to go deeper into Irish sources to learn more. My main intent has been to give a background for the understanding of Irish American Catholicism. For it is this nineteenth- and early-twentieth-century expression of the Catholic Church that was brought to the American shores. It was all a very recent Irish development and not the deeper Celtic Christian tradition of the people. Yes, much of their tradition lived on in the people's faith and personal religious practices. Unfortunately, however, the church often pitted itself against the old ways. Before we move on to look at the Irish American experience, I want to explore the more recent development of the church in Ireland.

Winds of Change

A high rate of emigration persisted well past the middle of the twentieth century because young people were unable to find work at home. Ireland was often characterized as a "third world" country in its poverty, and insufficient education and development. One has only to read Frank McCourt's best-seller, *Angela's Ashes*, to realize the extent of poverty and underdevelopment that still characterized sections of Ireland in the 1940s. Change, however, began to seep in after the Second World War, and became particularly evident by the 1960s.

Universal secondary education and many other educational possibilities became available to the Irish in the 1960s. Twenty years later, the next generation of Irish was said to be the best educated in all of Europe. The postwar affluence of America and other Western countries brought a new influx of tourists to Ireland, and with them came an exposure to the bigger world. The election of John Kennedy to the presidency of the United States in 1960 and his subsequent visit to Ireland enkindled the pride of all Irish Catholics. The development of the media, particularly of television, brought to the people of the Emerald Isle a further burgeoning awareness of bigger vistas. By the 1980s a cultural renaissance was afoot in Ireland. Music, art, cinema, drama, poetry — all these blossomed with new life. Seamus Heaney won a Nobel Prize for poetry. An awakening of the appreciation of Irish traditional music had occurred around 1951, when a group of musicians founded *Comhaltas Ceoltóirí Éireann,* to counter the face of the growing pop music trend, particular of the ballroom variety. Other musicians, such as the *Chieftains, DeDanaan, Altan,* and *Clannad,* soon made traditional music popular again. The *Clancy Brothers* and other groups in the United States brought an American and worldwide audience to this music. Still later, productions such as *Riverdance* appeared on the world stage and gave the outside world a new appreciation of things Celtic and Irish. The worldwide appreciation of Irish music gave the Irish a deeper pride in their own musical heritage.

With the exception of a few priests who strove to promote the Gaelic culture,[12] the mainstream church shared little of, nor was the cause of, this new outburst of life and pride. There was little in the church's educational offerings to parallel the educational advances in the general culture. The old ways had worked for so long. Why change anything? There were those who believed that the desire for change must indicate a loss of faith.

The prevalent cultural insularity began to give way when Ireland entered the European Economic Community. Cracks in the firm authority structure of the church emerged as debates raged over proposed referenda dealing with abortion, contraception, divorce, and homosexuality. A foreshadowing of this had occurred in 1951, when the Catholic hierarchy, under Archbishop McQuaid, squelched the attempts of Dr. Noel Browne, Minister of Health for Ireland, to initiate "mother and child" welfare legislation for a country that had the highest infant mortality rate in Europe. The bishops attacked the plan as socialist and undermining the rights of parents.

The vehement reaction of the bishops, leading to Browne's resignation, left a bad taste in the people's mouth in regard to the church. One writer believes that this display of naked authoritarianism was the beginning of the end of the church's special position in the Irish polity.[13] By the 1960s, as these controversial issues began to be aired, there was a sharp decline in the unquestioning obedience to the church, and many people no longer believed so surely in the certainty of the punishment of hell for many offenses, such as missing Mass on Sunday. Things came to a head in 1992 with the news that the bishop of Galway, Doctor Eamonn Casey, had fathered a child of an American woman and, while personally neglecting mother and child, had used church funds to support them. Bishop Casey had been a well-liked bishop and a good leader in social and educational programs. But this scandal let the steam out of the kettle, and accusations of hypocrisy and dishonesty on the part of clergy and of the church in general followed. A number of cases of pedophilia involving priests also followed, as well as stories of other kinds of abuses in church schools and orphanages. Disillusionment, disbelief, and anticlericalism, the last given publicity by the media and sometimes being of a highly virulent variety, soon were all part of the wake of this storm. The affluence of the 1990s led further to the abandonment of the church by many who were taken up by the advantages of a new secularist approach to Irish society.

Whither the Irish Church?

I am sure there are many different reactions to what is happening in the Irish church today. Some may see it as a tragedy. Others may see it as a welcome change and healthy development. No doubt, you can find both positive and negative elements in all of this unfolding. Irish society, though thriving economically, is also undergoing turmoil. Crime, drugs, and violence have become more common, especially in the cities. The ways of the Western nations of the "first world" have been embraced, and that has included some of the worst features of Western society in its greed and consumerist mentality. Perhaps most disturbing is the high rate of suicide. Ireland, according to the Archdiocese of Dublin in a March 1999 report, has the fastest-growing rate of youth suicide in the world, and almost one in four suicides occurs among young people, especially males, between the ages of fifteen and twenty-four. Alcoholism, depression, and other serious illnesses are some causes of this; other contributing factors are the emptiness and insecurity and confusion of changing roles and societal norms, as well as the terrible academic pressure for entrance into university that has followed universal education.

The church, in some sectors, continues to operate, often as though nothing has changed. The practice of the faith, as measured by church attendance, has plummeted. Though about 57 percent of Catholics still go to church, a very high number for any Western nation, this figure is down considerably from the close to 90 percent attendance of former years. Many Catholics, whether practicing or not, have been remarkably ignorant of their religion because of such inadequate and simplistic instruction in their faith. There are those who remain firmly dedicated to the practice of their faith but who are, in reality, very angry people, lashing out at the church, society, or whomever they can blame for their unresolved issues. I personally encountered some of these people when giving a talk in Dublin on the riches of Celtic Christianity. I listened patiently and tried to show understanding, for these people need healing too.

The present phase may be seen as growing pains and a sign that a new church is being born. There are many vital parishes and centers of the faith. The Catholic publishing industry turns out a great number of hope-filled and inspiring books and periodicals, which are being bought and read. Some of these publications record the faith journeys of people in these changing times in a poignant and loving way.[14] There is still a great deal of love for the church, even in those who find it wanting in so many ways. I received a personal letter from a former Irish Catholic priest that touched me in this regard. I share some of it here.

> I practiced as a Catholic diocesan priest for more than thirteen years. However, the arid clericalism of the present Catholic Church was just too much for me. I am now happily married, but still seeking a spirituality which is relevant in a secular Ireland. The Celtic Tiger has replaced the monk's cat. As I look around, it's sad to see so much of our heritage being lost to the new gods of shopping and business. And still there is hope. I believe you have identified the sources of this hope. Personally I am convinced that if spirituality is to survive and flourish, the best road to go is to return to our roots and experience the wealth of faith, of understanding, life, meaning and laughter which is our heritage. The challenge then is to express this in a language and symbol which will touch the minds, hearts and souls of our people. Surely we have the answers all around us in the sea, earth, people, music and even the pubs (as you so correctly identified), but how can we take away all the masks and screens to let the Lord's light shine through?

Others in Ireland are taking up this challenge and reclaiming their own deeper heritage. Holy wells are still places of prayer. Pilgrimages to Croagh Patrick, Lough Derg, and other sacred sites are more popular than ever. Old Celtic places are being revived as retreat centers in Glendalough, Dingle, Balintubber Abbey, Kildare, and elsewhere.[15] Within the church, voices are now being raised in writing, speaking, and acting, calling for the re-integration of the Celtic tradition with the practice of the Catholic faith. There are priests such as Father Pat Ahern, who has furthered the Celtic consciousness by his work with *Siamsa Tíre,* a folk theater group based in Tralee, County Kerry, building on the old Celtic myths and stories. The recovery of the Celtic imagination and tradition as well as the Irish language enhances this re-integration of faith and culture. A positive and hopeful view was expressed by Father Colm Kilcoyne of western Ireland.

> I suggest that this is where the vast majority of church members stands right now: wanting the church to be relevant; wishing their children to continue in the tradition; prepared to look beyond the scandals and the amateurism; willing the church out of its tiredness into some kind of vision that will give meaning to a jumbled and hectic new Ireland; aching for a simplicity that connects them with Jesus Christ.[16]

In this chapter I have tried to be realistic about both the negative effects of the past and the positive hope for the future as I described the present state of Irish Catholicism. Ireland, more so than America, may have deeper roots to call on for a successful transition. The land, the air, the language, and the traditional faith that have been part of a living culture all stand as a strong witness to the possibility of a church that can once again adapt. I suspect that secularism and affluence present more of a threat to the faith than do the years of colonial domination. Perhaps things will get worse in some places before they can get better. But there is hope, and the signs are that many are grabbing on to that hope to build a new Irish Catholic synthesis for tomorrow. I expect that my Irish grandparents would have been among them.

Chapter Three

Irish American Catholicism

*M*Y IRISH GRANDPARENTS, after immigrating to America, were married in a church in downtown Manhattan. They soon settled in an area of Brooklyn where my father was born. When my father married my mother, also a Brooklynite, they moved over the line to nearby Queens County. Though my mother had come from an Austrian background, she was known as Kitty, and many people thought she was Irish. She certainly embraced the Irish ethos in religion, culture, music, and so forth. Dad was the first president of the Holy Name Society of the newly established parish of the Sacred Heart of Jesus in East Glendale. The neighborhood was largely composed of German and Irish second-generational families. The pastor was German, but the practices of this church were certainly in the Irish mold. I grew up in this place and was thoroughly indoctrinated in the Catholic culture of the time. Attendance at Sunday Mass was an inviolable obligation. Regular "going to confession" was a necessity. I went to a Catholic school and was an altar boy at the church. Weekly novena nights in honor of Our Lady of Perpetual Help and the Sacred Heart of Jesus were well attended. Lenten Stations of the Cross, yearly Forty Hours Devotion, the annual mission, May crowning of the statue of Mary—I can remember them all. We lived safely in an enclosed and secure world. We were not allowed to go into a Protestant church or even to attend the YMCA. Social events were held in the parish too, and these included the "minstrel," in which black-faced parishioners made great fun of another culture. I think that the minstrel was particularly common in Irish parishes. The youth of the parish were active in the CYO (Catholic Youth Organization), and all sorts of athletic and social events were available for them.

How did this all come about, this coherent subculture of church? Priests and nuns, in their otherworldly clothes, were a particularly obvious and symbolic manifestation of this culture. Now I realize that our Protestant and Jewish neighbors marveled at this system. And now I also realize that this development was a deliberate choice. The relation of American Catholics to the rest of the culture could have been much different if some Catholic pioneers had had their way. We will consider that other way, which was considered at the time of the great immigrations. The decision to construct this separate culture was a conscious and willful decision, and the model for it went back to Archbishop Paul Cullen and the postfamine Irish Catholic Church.

A Church of Immigrants

In the year 2000 the Catholic population of the United States accounts for roughly between one-fifth and one-fourth of the entire country. It is the largest religious group in America. It is hard for us to realize that this was predominantly a Protestant country in its inception, molded by Protestant values and ways. In the 1830s there were, at most, six hundred thousand Catholics in the United States, and these were a mixture of French, German, Irish, English, Portuguese, and Spanish. Nineteenth-century immigration would change that as numerous groups of Catholics arrived from various European countries. In the latter part of the century large groups of Italians, Poles, Germans, and other Europeans would disembark from sailing ships onto American shores. But the Irish would put their particular mark on this new Catholic presence in the New World for two reasons. First, they were the first group to arrive in large numbers. Second, a good many of them (though not all at first) spoke the English language. By 1890, American Catholics numbered seven million — the largest denomination in the country — at that time representing about 12.5 percent of the total population. Yes, the Irish were making their predominance felt in this new Catholic Church that was emerging.

Throughout the world the Irish influence on the nineteenth-century church was out of proportion to its numbers. In 1869, seventy-three of the bishops at the First Vatican Council, 10 percent of the total assembly, were Irish, and bishops of Irish descent throughout the world raised this number to 20 percent. In the United States the percentage was even larger. Between 1850 and 1880, half of all newly consecrated American bishops were Irish. This number grew to 60 percent in 1890 and then remained at 75 percent throughout the first half of the twentieth century. Nine out of ten seminarians at major American seminaries in the latter part of the nine-teenth century were Irish. This was an ethnic group, we recall, that came as dedicated churchgoers, unlike many anticlerical immigrants from other European countries. So it was that as late as the 1970s, when Irish Americans represented less than one-fifth of the American Catholic Church, one-third of the clergy in general, and one-half of the hierarchy in particular, were Irish.[17]

The Irishness of the American Church

From what we have seen above, we know how this Irish presence would be expressed. The nineteenth-century

Irish church of devotions, discipline and law, strong dedi-
cation and loyalty to the priests and nuns, and a morality
focused on the prohibitions about sexuality in the sixth
commandment were all part of this church in America.
Generally speaking, the Irish immigrants who arrived
were extremely poor and uneducated. They left an im-
poverished country behind and many died on the "coffin
ships" that brought them here. Once here, they sometimes
faced equally dire conditions in the cities in which they
settled — New York, Boston, New Orleans — as well as in
smaller enclaves in the Midwest,[18] and a strange thing occurred at this point. Attempts were made to move the Irish
into rural situations that would have been more like what
they were used to in Ireland. Bishop Benedict Fenwick
in Boston attempted to settle many newly arrived immigrants in idyllic farm situations in Maine. Bishop John
Ireland tried to do the same in Minnesota. A few Irish
moved into the wilder, unsettled areas of the West. But
the great majority of the immigrants stayed in the cities.[19]
The conditions and habitations in which they lived were
ghettolike. Overcrowding of large families and clans was
a common occurrence. Men took the most menial positions as laborers. Women were often in a better situation,
taking live-in positions doing domestic work in well-to-do
Yankee homes, thus learning the ways of the new culture
from within.[20]

When we ask what kept these insecure and impov-
erished people together, we discover that it was the
parish. The local church and its geographical territory
became the substitute for the small village left behind.
One's identity was found in belonging to the parish. This
type of belonging continued on for many decades. Irish
American Catholics became accustomed to introducing
themselves as "I'm from Saint Kevin's" or "I'm from
Saint Theresa's" rather than from their identifiable area
or neighborhood. In turn, this contributed to the parish

becoming a self-enclosed enclave offering a number of services to its people — spiritual, educational, social, athletic, and economic. Everything was centered in the parish, and people's lives were often confined to it. Evening devotions, communion breakfasts, socials and dances, and CYO events for the young were all part of this pattern. Catholic newspapers and magazines flourished. A "Legion of Decency" protected Catholics in their movie viewing. The temperance movement begun in Ireland by Father Theobold Matthew was foisted on the young as a means to forestall the evils of drink. Other than for work, there was little need to go outside of the parish. And the employment that most Irish took on was in the civil services, such as police, fire, and sanitation departments, where they would find security and be with other Irish Catholics. And, of course, the Catholic school became the linchpin of this parish. Terry Golway, writing in *The Irish in America*, sums up the parish phenomenon in these words:

> For more than a century, the parish was as central to the organization of urban life in heavily Catholic cities as any government institution. The parish was the place no hostile culture and no offensive custom could penetrate. The sons and daughters of immigrant parents met under the auspices of the parish, and those who married often did so in the building where they had been baptized. The pace of parish life was set by the liturgical calendar — individual months were dedicated to certain devotions (The Sacred Heart, Saint Joseph), Saturday evenings were set aside for confessions, and an assortment of Holy Days and First Fridays called parishioners to additional worship. The local fish market was crowded with neighbors every Friday morning. Families with the variety of problems that afflicted the poor and

the alienated turned to the parish priest, whose training for such social work was uneven at best. The
parish was a world of common values and shared
rituals.[21]

Another aspect of this separatist community was a certain suspicion of learning that was even anti-intellectual
at times. A small and sheltered worldview and an un-
awareness of other peoples and cultures contributed to
a dark side of the Irish Catholic culture, one that was
often expressed in biases and prejudices not only against
Protestants, but blacks and Jews as well. Some Catholics
were aware of this mindset, and criticism of the closed-
mindedness of the Catholic worldview can be found in
writers such as George Schuster and in the lay-edited
Commonweal magazine. The most respected Catholic institution of higher learning was the University of Notre
Dame in Indiana. Although founded by French clergy,
it soon developed an Irish identity, was vocal in its fur-
thering of Irish nationalism abroad, and was best known
among American Catholics for its "Fighting Irish" foot-
ball team. But it would be a long time before any
great numbers of Irish Americans attended school on the
university level.

Looking back at this whole development, it is somewhat revealing to uncover that all of this might have
developed quite differently. There were two schools of
thought among the American bishops of how to help
incorporate all these immigrants, whether Irish or any
other ethnic group. John Ireland was born in Connemara,
County Galway, in 1838 and he immigrated into the
United States in 1849. Eventually he became the archbishop of Minneapolis and Saint Paul. He emerged as the
leader of a group of American bishops who believed in
the integration of the Irish, as well as all Catholics, into
the mainstream of American society. He believed in the

need for them to become good American citizens by fully taking part in this new land, including going to the public schools. This point of view did not look upon Protestants with any suspicion or hostility, but rather, believed that Catholics could live and work with them.

The contrary view was held by Archbishop Hughes of New York. John Joseph Hughes was a native of Ulster in Northern Ireland, born in County Tyrone in 1797, who immigrated into the new land in 1830. Becoming the first archbishop of New York in 1850, his own background of being a Catholic minority in Northern Ireland was manifested in how he conducted the church. He was tireless in safeguarding Irish Catholics against the encroachment of the Protestant majority by keeping them as separated as possible. Hughes stood up for the rights of his people, even threatening the Protestant majority with revolution if they did not respect the Catholics. One of his first statements in New York was to predict that Catholics would conquer America. He was known as Dagger John, from the custom of bishops signing a cross before their signatures, which looked like a stiletto to the Yankee natives. He was a strong man who gave some sense of dignity to his flock by focusing on their Catholic identity and insisting that they stay close to the church as he championed the education, work conditions, and civil rights of his flock. Archbishop William O'Connell in Boston (1912–44), Archbishop Dennis Dougherty in Philadelphia (1918–31), and many others would follow his example in this vein. John Ireland's vision faded away and was often associated with the pseudo-heresy of "Americanism," which Vatican authorities feared was developing in America. Thus the Irish model of Paul Cullen, intensified again in mid-century Ireland under John Charles McQuaid, took root in America. This has been well summed up by historian Charles Morris:

The enveloping formalism of the American Church sprang from the Cullen/Hughes recipe for upgrading Irish peasant immigrant hoards — go to Mass, receive the sacraments, send your children to Catholic schools, do as the nuns and priests say, give money, avoid drunkenness and impurity. Such mandates implied an imposing and far-flung services network, playing to the strength of Irish-American prelates, who were hardheaded businessmen and practical politicians rather than theologians.[22]

Bishops in the mold of John Hughes led the American church for the next century. Even bishops who were not Irish, such as Cardinal George Mundelein, archbishop of Chicago (1915–39), held up the Irish model of church as the standard. All of Mundelein's auxiliary bishops, by the way, were chosen from the Irish! Thus the Irish character of the American Catholic Church took firm root and flourished for some time to come.

The "Irish Catholic" in America

If being Irish and Catholic had become synonymous back in Ireland, a new hybrid developed in America. The Irish in their new setting continued to think of themselves as Irish but gradually became unaware of how different things had become. We can begin to discern the spiritual aspects of this new church by examining the spiritual worldview of these Irish American Catholics. The great majority of them arrived during and after the famine. They left behind a horrendous scene, a very painful and tragic one. For many of them it was something much too painful to confront. A good deal of denial and romantic distancing ensued for first- and second-generation Irish Americans. There was a strong component of guilt too — guilt for surviving while many died, guilt for leaving behind one's country and family. Most of these immigrants never went home again. Some sent money back. Some wrote. Others just tried to forget the past. They did not discuss the Ireland they left behind with their children but emphasized becoming Americans. In time, any talk of the "auld sod" was a sentimentalized talk of leprechauns, of always being a happy and joking people, of their great capacity to down a few pints of beer — in short, memories of a land of fantasies and dreams and visions of a land that no one really knew or ever visited. Saint Patrick's Day was celebrated by wearing green, singing Tin Pan Alley songs such as "When Irish Eyes Are Smiling," and by much drinking. Sad to say, this mindset still persists. Stereotypes of Irish drinking have prevailed as sources of jokes and greeting cards. When visiting a Catholic college recently, I was told that they had held a Saint Patrick's Day celebration the night before. The "votive offerings" for this holy feast littered the campus in the form of discarded beer cans!

Another trait of this immigrant group was a high need for respectability. The shame at not having enough food to feed one's family or to be hospitable to others in need had to be endured and covered up in the famine. Many starving people were too proud to accept free help from others, and Irish Americans continued to exhibit this need for respectability. Things had to look right. The Irish had to look good before the English. Irish Americans had to look good before the Yankee Protestants. Children had to be well behaved in public. Lace curtains in the windows are often a symbol of this mindset. No one must know the family business, that Daddy drinks or Johnny has married outside the church. Secrets abounded, and with keeping secrets there always comes shame. A good deal of dysfunctionalism in such families became the norm.[23]

Because the famine was such a painful and traumatic experience, its effects remained buried in the unconscious for many years. Only with the 150th anniversary of this tragedy in 1995–98 were adequate attempts made to look at this historical happening and to understand how it left scars both in Ireland and among Irish immigrants in other countries. Only now are we beginning to understand what spiritual and emotional baggage many have been carrying around with them. It is this kind of baggage that I have alluded to in the beginning of this book as needing the healing and freedom that leads to reconciliation both within an individual and in his or her relations to others.

Rather than describe all this in detail, I refer the reader to some popular attempts to deal with the topic. A number of films in the past ten years have dramatically portrayed the human stories of Irish people hurt by the past. The contrast of these recent films with earlier attempts in the cinema to portray the Irish community is significant. The earlier ones were light and healthy in tone, as well as being very sentimental. *The Quiet Man* portrayed the Ireland of a young American coming back to his ancestor's home as a delightful and jovial place to which to return. Bing Crosby as Father Chuck O'Malley in *Going My Way,* Spencer Tracy in *Boys Town,* and Karl Malden in *On the Waterfront* all portrayed Irish American priests as strong, manly, and well respected.

More recent plays and films about the Irish have been much more nuanced and not always light and cheerful. Brian Friel's award-winning play, *Dancing at Lughnasa,* which also became a film, showed the depressive type of village life that still existed in the late 1940s in Donegal in Ireland. Five unhappy spinster sisters and a brother, a disillusioned priest returning from Africa, live out the narrow understanding of life and religion that still prevailed. A later film, *This Is My Father,* a story taking place in the 1930s in County Galway, shows the same prevalent sad and narrow morality. In this story a lonely and hard-working man hangs himself in despair after being condemned for his sexual liaison with a young woman. More recent Irish immigrants who have seen these movies remember the circumstances as true and factual. They can laugh at them now and distance themselves from the pain. Laughter and humor have often been the means of the Irish to distance themselves from feeling too deeply the pain of many situations.

The dysfunctional Irish American Catholic world has also been portrayed on the silver screen. *The Brothers McMullen* is a low-budget film made by Ed Burns in the mid-1990s that reflects his own growing up in Queens, New York. Three brothers enact their own stories — their difficulties with love and commitment, their guilt about love and sex, and their legalistic loyalty to the church. A sequel to that film, *She's the One,* also explored the New York Irish American family, with its confusions surrounding belief and morality. Perhaps a more serious film was *Good Will Hunting,* about a young man, talented but also troubled, from the Irish enclave in South Boston. The youth is realistically portrayed as fearful of, and even feeling incapable of, breaking out of his ghetto existence, unhappy but unable to do anything about it, using alcohol and violence to cope. "Southie," as it is called, continues to be an area with a high suicide rate among its youth, some of whom find life unbearable and think their own lives to be meaningless.[24] As is often the case, these poor have been put down and abused by various government and social groups, including the Irish who have made it elsewhere.

Much of this represents the negative side of the Irish American experience. Of course, there were positive aspects too. There are many stories of great heroism and profound faith among people who overcame huge obstacles and made successes of their lives. The Irish have done more than their share in helping to build America. I have looked at the dark side, though, because it needs to be recognized, acknowledged, and let go of in order for healing to take place. Denial and indiscriminate projection, on others or on institutions, need to be set aside. Blame needs to be turned into understanding and compassion for those who went before us and who were, possibly, even more hurt than we ever were.

The Irish as Patriot

There is one special area of Irish American Catholicism that I want to address. I have pointed out the separatist, almost ghettolike, existence that Catholic parishes represented. There were separate schools, athletic teams, professional societies, and so forth. But there is one area in which the American Catholic has tended to be at the center of the American experience. That is as patriot. Perhaps as a way to feel accepted, perhaps as a way to prove they were really Americans, Irish Catholics have been patriotic to the point of a sometimes reactionary and conservative adherence to "my country, right or wrong, but my country." They have been on the front lines as volunteers for the armed services in many wars. They have also been very visible in the public service as police and firefighters. The FBI has recruited heavily from the Irish in past years. They were rabidly anti-Communist during the Cold War. Until the election of John Kennedy as president, the Irish always felt the need to defend themselves against charges of a primary loyalty to a foreign authority in the person of the pope. As late as 1949 Paul Blanchard was making serious accusations about American Catholics being subject to the pope and therefore not true Americans. In 1960 John Kennedy had to face the same criticism while campaigning for the American presidency.[25]

Some of this again touches another aspect of the dark side of the Irish American story, mentioned earlier in the context of Catholic anti-intellectualism. The Irish were on the frontline of opposition to the military conscription of citizens for the Union Army in the American Civil War. Many Catholics, knowingly or not, abetted a racist attitude toward blacks. Fearful of slaves being freed and moving into the open job market, the Irish reacted with an antiemancipation attitude. The year 1863 in New York City was marked by racial civil strife in which 105 people died and thousands were injured. There were at least a half a dozen blacks who were publicly lynched. The Irish played a large part in this story, and this too has hung in the psyche needing to be healed. The irony was that the Irish were much like the blacks in how they lived both in Ireland and in their first years in America. Frederick Douglass, who himself had been a slave, in visiting Ireland during the famine, saw the Irish suffering similarly to his fellow slaves in America. Irish and blacks shared similar experiences. But the Irish needed to prove themselves as Americans and, in doing so, prove themselves to be really "white."[26] A chasm developed. Well into the twentieth century the church itself did nothing to encourage integration, nor did Rome ever offer any condemnation of slavery.

A Time for Healing

Those who have experienced any of the above need no further details. Many no longer want any part of the old church, which was so closed, narrow minded, and at times intolerant of moral failures amongst its own members within and intolerant of non-Catholics outside its walls. But much of this church was only a last-century development. There is a bigger story to uncover, and I have heard from many people who are grateful to discover that there is a larger story in which to insert their own life's stories.

Joanne, a young American woman studying in Dublin, is a graduate student doing research on depression, manic depression, and problem drinking among the Irish. Her own studies were proving to be personally healing, and she wrote to thank me for my book in these words:

> I myself have had similar experiences of finally understanding childhood events. Suddenly certain parental behaviors become explicable when understood within a larger framework. And the experience was both healing and liberating as you described.

So we do not need to be afraid to name the darkness and bring the past into the light. The past cannot destroy the present or the future. Furthermore, as we all recognize sooner or later, each of us has a story that is a combination of light and darkness. Nor is it just my own personal story. I am part of a bigger story whether I realize it or not. As Americans, we often tend to think that history has just begun with us, and so we believe that we are free to choose any direction, belief, value, or future that we wish. But freedom has to be won; it is not just given. The past gives us both help and misdirection. Sorting it all out is part of each person's own journey, but it cannot be done alone.

Before going on to describe how claiming our deeper Celtic roots can bring healing, and before looking at how the real Celtic tradition might bring new light and meaning to the Irish Catholic, I will complete my survey by showing how the old church has come apart. This will bring us to the present, where the healing must take place.

Chapter Four

From Certainty
to Confusion

I WAS ORDAINED a Catholic priest in 1959. When, not too long ago, I celebrated my fortieth anniversary, my brother brought out my mother's album of photographs taken at my ordination and first Mass. It was humorous to look at pictures of our younger selves. How we have changed and, even more striking, how our culture has changed! Looking back, the 1960s now appear as a great divide separating us from another world. That album is a bit of history, a period piece, a memory of a time now passed. I have looked at pictures of my parents taken in the 1920s, and they don't seem as remote in time and culture as do the pictures of the 1950s.

In the photos of my first Mass, I stand facing the altar with my back to the people and with a deacon and sub-deacon placed in a formal line behind me. I never looked directly at the people, even when turning around to greet them. I am wearing the old "fiddle back" narrow type Mass vestment (a "chasuble") and a lace alb. Of course, the photo doesn't tell you that everything was said in Latin, but I certainly remember that. Just as interesting are the images of the rest of the people. All the women wear small, flowery hats. All the men have military type hair-cuts. This uniformity was symbolic of the age. It wasn't just the church that was a fixed and unchanging institution, as well as being a distinctive subculture of its own. The national culture was also very set in its post–world war ways. Domestically, the Eisenhower years may have seemed to be placid years of well-being, peace, and prosperity, when all seemed well with America. On the foreign front, communism loomed as a threat, but this only made the inner coherence of the nation stronger in its patriotic identity. But, right beneath the surface lay many problematic areas that would all surface in the 1960s.

A New, Mobile Generation

By the middle of the twentieth century, the Catholic Church, so solid and monolithic throughout the world, had developed a successful and triumphant presence in the New World. So much of this institution and subculture would collapse in the 1960s and ensuing years. This took many by complete surprise, and there were those who reacted with anger and demands for a return to the simple faith of yesteryear. Others saw the collapse as justifying their own views of a church that had become too powerful and even hypocritical in its use of power and control. In still others, it started a new journey in faith to understand and comprehend what had happened and to find what God might be saying to them in the second half of the twentieth century.

Thus the 1960s were a watershed time for American culture in general and for the American Catholic Church in particular. The Second Vatican Council (1962–65) changed many attitudes and positions of the church, though not its doctrines. Many blame the Council for the resultant decrease of faith in and loyalty to the church. But the ground had already begun to shift much before this, and the old church was already doomed to undergo change, if not collapse. A key factor affecting the Western world was a new mobility of people, and with this mobility came a new awareness of the bigger world around them. This probably had already begun with the First World War as America was brought out of its isolation into contact with diverse cultures, nationalities, and religious groups. A shift of people away from the inner cities had already begun in the 1930s and 1940s, but any appreciable social change was diminished by the Great Depression. Even those who moved in those years, such as my own parents, who moved from Brooklyn out to Queens on Long Island, continued to live a local, neighborhood-centered life. The parish church, school, and social activities dominated much of life. It was only after the Second World War that dramatic change really occurred.

The movement of large groups of people out of the cities into the new suburbs was a major social development of the times. And with that movement the very fabric of American Catholicism was altered. The all-inclusive parish that was the center of people's lives began to change, at first imperceptibly, but change nonetheless. People began to move and change jobs more frequently. Airplane travel became popular. Television opened up a new world. At first, those Catholics who were among the first to move to the suburbs often still felt connected to the parish of their childhood. Their very identity had been rooted in a place. After moving, they often went back to "their" parish for special occasions (and always expected that it remain there for them when needed!). Many were not even aware that, although they had departed, they still carried the mindset of its life with them. But their children would never know such a place or life. The old separatist parish was gone.

A second major cultural shift that affected Catholics, along with other middle-class groups, was the postwar GI Bill of Rights, which opened up higher education, for the first time, to the sons and daughters of poor immigrants.

Irish Catholics, like many other immigrant groups, had been mostly blue-collar workers, satisfied with a good high school education and a decent job. The GI Bill resulted in an educational explosion and a fantastic one-generational jump took place. In the 1950s there were few Irish Americans with higher education, but in the 1970s the Irish emerged as nearly the best-educated ethnic group in the United States (second only to the Jewish population), as the group with the most college-educated and doctoral graduates.[27] Personally, I owe the possibility of a higher education to the church and going to a seminary. I probably am the first of the Joyce line to have gone to college. My great-grandfather could not write, and I can vividly remember seeing his X written in the marriage register of the Irish documents. When my grandfather, who was a laborer, died from an accident on the job in a Brooklyn cemetery, my father left school at the age of twelve to take care of his mother. My own mother went to a two-year secretarial school after grade school, as did many girls in her time. My brother continued this direction and went into the world of business after high school and then into the military during the Korean War. I know what education has meant to all of us second-generation Irish Americans.

I have heard stories of people being chastised as children for asking questions. Knowledge, in some families, was considered to be dangerous. Perhaps there was shame at one's ignorance and lack of education. It was simpler just to be expected to accept what your elders tell you. Be obedient. Simply believe! If there is a problem encountered, just offer it up! That was still the ethos of the church, the seminary, and probably most of the nation in the 1950s. But, with education comes reflection and questions. The old ways no longer work. The Catholic laity today is an intelligent group of people who read and think and discuss. We now live in a different world. This is not a condemnation of the older world, for people of those times often led heroic lives, achieving much with very little resources. In such a sea of change, demands for a new and different church have also come about.

The Sixties Revolution

It is always difficult to pinpoint one exact time or event that altered the tide of history. The Catholic Church had already begun to change, as we have seen, due to the movement of many to the suburbs and the ensuing break-down of the inner-city closed community. But there were other signs of change as well. The perception in the minds of other Americans of the Catholic as non-American out-sider was now giving way to a perception of Catholic respectability and acceptability. One indication of this was the wide acclaim given to a book, *The Seven Storey Mountain,* written by a Catholic monk, Thomas Merton. Published by Harcourt, Brace and Company in October of 1948, the book went through numerous printings to become a best-seller. The book echoed a new, postwar search for meaning. In this autobiography of one man's conversion to Catholicism and his commitment to monas-ticism, readers experienced a spiritual and intellectual dimension to Catholicism previously unrecognized. The author's telling of his search for meaning through various ways of the world resonated with many people personally. By the 1960s, this reclusive monk had touched countless others through his books, letters, and poetry.

A still more popular expression of Catholicism, reach-ing countless millions, was Bishop Fulton J. Sheen's long-running television program, *Life Is Worth Living.* From February 1952 through mid-1957, "Uncle Ful-tie" educated and delighted his viewers with Catholic (and anti-Communist) doctrine and stories.[28] Here was a charismatic Catholic, and a priest at that, who communicated faith and religious conviction in a joyful and disarming manner.

The event, however, that really changed the position of the American Catholic, especially the Irish Catholic, was the election in 1960 of John Fitzgerald Kennedy as the first Roman Catholic American president. Beyond the political significance of his presidency, the man stands out as an icon, a great symbol of the final arrival of the Irish in America. He gave to both the Irish in the old country and to the immigrant community in the United States a dignity and acceptance that they had never experienced under the English or American Protestant majority. His picture still hangs in many Irish homes. His visit to Ireland in 1963 was a spectacular homecoming event that abetted the Irish in their own coming home to their sense of dignity and worth. The Irish Catholic community in the United States, hitherto so separate and apart, no longer had to prove themselves real Americans. A part of the old impetus to remain in tight communities and remain apart from the mainstream was now dissipated. But there is still a great irony in this event. Kennedy has been called the most secular of American presidents to date, for his predecessors had all vigorously upheld the Protestant tradition. But his self-defense against the accusations of being under a foreign authority — meaning the pope — and his avowed freedom to follow his own conscience, reinforced and strengthened the growing public tendency to make religion a totally private matter, not something to be paraded in the public square. The old doctrine of separation of church and state would come to mean that private and moral values could be divorced from the public areas of life.

In the previous century, the Catholic Church had rejected any accommodation to the American culture and had opted for a totally separate existence. Now, in the second half of the twentieth century, Catholics would be brought fully into the mainstream culture. Is this what Archbishop Ireland and others of his viewpoint wanted? Is this what Archbishop John Hughes had wanted to avoid? It is difficult to know what might have been the outcome if Ireland's school of thought had prevailed a century before. But for now, the pressure of loyalty and fidelity to the Catholic ethos, doctrines, and rules would be lessened and considered as no longer really necessary for personal identity and survival.

The Second Vatican Council (1962–65) took place, for American Catholics, against this larger background. The worldwide gathering of bishops in Rome brought about significant changes, particularly in language, ritual, and practices, such as Mass in the vernacular tongue with the priest facing the people, the suspension of the need to abstain from meat on Friday, and the introduction of laypeople into areas of worship and parish life hitherto reserved for ordained priests. More significantly, it promoted an attitude of openness to the world that the Vatican had seemingly condemned only a century before. The fearful suspicion of modernity, of democracy, and of religious tolerance had all been clearly expressed by Pope Pius IX (1846–70) in his so-called *Syllabus of Errors*. Now the Second Vatican Council declared the church to be servant to the world.

> The joys and hopes, the grief and anguish of the people of our time, especially of those who are poor or afflicted, are the joys and hopes, the grief and anguish of the followers of Christ as well. Nothing that is genuinely human fails to find an echo in their hearts.[29]

I look back to the 1960s and recall so much that was exhilarating and promising but never bore fruit. There was a call to generosity, service, and community. Good leadership might have taken us elsewhere than where we actually went. The assassination of President Kennedy was a traumatic national event followed by the morass of the Vietnam War. A great distrust of authority and government spilled over to the church and it was only aggravated by the ensuing Watergate affair. All of this affected the Catholic community. Polarization of conservatives and liberals now began to be a constant occurrence in discussions of politics, education, and religion. The old Catholic monolithic system had crumbled and become nonexistent.

The Seventies Revival

The "sixties revolution" was fueled by a crisis in identity. The call to patriotism no longer stirred the heart or elicited the consensus and response that it once did. Loyalty to the church no longer united Catholics. Since so much of the previous Cullen-Hughes recipe for Catholic identity rested on a separation from, and often an antipathy toward, Protestants, the new tolerance for diversity meant a distillation of identity for many. Large numbers of Catholic priests and nuns abandoned their particular calling. New vocations dwindled. Catholic life, as exemplified in regular attendance at Sunday Mass and the practice of regular confession, fell off dramatically. A crisis in church authority erupted in 1968 after Pope Paul VI issued his encyclical *Humanae Vitae,* "On Human Life." Contrary to the expectations of many, this document upheld the absolute ban against artificial contraception. Open rebellion, once a taboo for the Catholic community, rocked the church. The eventual reaction of the church authorities would be a lack of tolerance for any expression of differences and dissension. Lack of confidence in the church escalated when more and more stories of pedophilia and other sexual failings among priests, brothers, and nuns became known. A real crisis of authority and leadership became widespread.

As I reflect on the crisis in identity, it appears that the religious identity of Americans before the 1960s had replaced the ethnic identity of Europeans. Catholic togetherness and separation from the rest of the culture, for instance, gave the same kind of cohesiveness that an ethnic group would have had in Europe. The weakening of religious identity brought about an interesting return to older ethnic and national expressions as the center of sense of identity. Immigrants to America had previously accepted the "melting pot" theory and believed that their old national and ethnic roots were no longer important. Now they were simply "Americans." As a young boy, I tended to believe this, for this was what I had been taught. My parents, raised by their immigrant parents, knew little of their ancestral heritage and fully embraced the American scene. Oh yes, there were national celebrations, especially for the Irish. Saint Patrick's Day was a big event, but much of the celebration was centered on the achievements of the Irish immigrants in the New World. As mentioned previously, the trappings of shamrocks, green clothes, beer, and leprechauns, all part of the mythology of this event, reflected very little of life in the old country.

The 1970s, however, inaugurated the first real interest in looking back and understanding the authentic Ireland whence parents or grandparents had come. Secure now in their American identity, Irish Americans responded to the *Roots* phenomenon that attracted so many Americans who wanted to explore their genetic and cultural background. Blacks, still called "Negroes" by many at the time, now began to take pride in their African background as "Afro-Americans." The same thing happened to Irish Americans. A better-educated generation now wanted to study and understand the Irish country of their forebears. Irish studies programs in language, music, art, and history began to be developed in settings such as the Jesuits' Boston College and the Holy Cross Fathers' Stonehill College, both in Massachusetts, as well as at Notre Dame University in Indiana. Because of the privatization of religion in America, however, Celtic religion and personal spirituality never became much of a component of these programs. Complementing these university classes, Irish cultural centers were developed in New York City, Boston, Minnesota, and in many other places.

Irish Catholics Today

Today, the Irish American community is a well-educated and mostly affluent group. Glossy magazines, such as *Irish America* and *The World of Hibernia*, publish regular stories of successful and respected Irish Americans in business, entertainment, athletics, education, and sometimes religion as well. A number of these newer Irish Americans travel back to Ireland now and enjoy the country, people, pubs, and golf courses.

And what of their spiritual lives? As I stated at the beginning of this book, many are restless and searching. Many continue their adherence to the Catholic Church, while some have joined other Christian churches. In many ways they have become like most other middle-class Americans. Both those who remain in the church and those who have left the church continue to search in many ways. Many women are angry at a male-dominated church and are demanding that their feminine voice be heard. Fewer men than women are actually involved in church or religion, some of them continuing to attend church for their wives' or families' sake. The problem of the alienation of males from religion has yet to be adequately addressed. There are certainly many vibrant parishes, but it is usually a small proportion of parishioners who are truly active. Passivity in both worship and church involvement is the norm for a great number of practicing Catholics. Many parishes have emphasized the education of children and have not reached out to the needs of older parishioners, other than getting the children's parents to come to church. Despite the very clear teachings of the church, divorce, contraception, and abortion are practiced at the same rate by Catholics as by the rest of the American populace. The large number of American Catholics, in itself, is certainly no indication of religious conviction and faith commitment.

So I come back to those who are really searching, to those for whom their native Catholicism stills holds at least some enticing memories. I am concerned for those who want a deeper spiritual life but don't know whether the church supports them in this desire. I hope that the survey in the past chapters has raised awareness of what has been lost and the reasons for the loss and confusion. If we can accept that times have changed, that the culture has gone through a mammoth shift, and that the old ways are insufficient, then I believe one is ready to explore ways to reappropriate one's Catholic tradition in a new way. Paradoxically, I believe that the new way is to go back to our Celtic roots. In opening ourselves to the spiritual worldview of the Celtic Christian of a millennium ago, we may be finding a point of view that allows us to live more spiritual and fruitful lives in the third millennium of Christianity.

Chapter Five

Choosing the Path to Healing

I NEVER GOT TO KNOW my father very well, as he died when I was twenty-six. I had been away at school for many years previous to that. I had known instinctively, however, that he was a hurt and scarred man. I tended to feel sorry for him, while wanting him to be stronger and more fatherly. His own scarred masculinity passed on to me something of a "father wound." Now, after some reflection on his Irish background, I can understand his parents a lot better, knowing both their struggle in Ireland and from whence they came. Likewise, I now understand better the story of their life as immigrants in this country, what they brought, both mentally and spiritually, with them to this country from Ireland. And that knowledge has led me to a better understanding of my father. I can understand, forgive, and love my own father so much more. And, in so doing, I love and forgive myself. We are all so intimately interwoven and our life is a web woven by and with others.

A PBS television series on New York City featured, as one of its four episodes, an account of the many immigrant waves to come to that city from Europe. In viewing this program, I was touched by a reflection by Peter Hamill, a New York writer. He recalled hearing his Irish-born father crying during the night. A feeling of sadness of having left his native country, his native language, and his family and friends left the father with a painful scar that he never felt free to show his family by day. He owed it to them to keep things going and offer them a new life in the New World. But Hamill observed that, upon hearing his father, he knew then that it was his obligation "to honor my father's pain." I find that moving and profound. To honor our parents' and ancestors' pain is to get our heart in touch with theirs and understand them in their own context. It may mean forgiving them for what they could not give us, or for the inadequate ideas and inadequate religious, educational, cultural, and even psychological formation that they handed down to us.

The healing of old wounds comes as a welcome relief to people who hitherto had not even suspected that their own pain was shared by others and that it could find release. A woman from Canada wrote to me, after reading my book,

> You have given me a spiritual awakening — a realization of deeper emotions and reasons for certain actions and attitudes which I was not aware of. . . . I am learning to love myself as well as my neighbors without feeling guilty, and also learning to understand other people, especially family members. I loved your description of the Irish race with all its mysticism and how it feels to be an Irish-American — or Irish-Canadian — no difference there.

The previous chapters have summarized the story, our story, the history of what our parents, grandparents, and ancestors have experienced. Without knowledge of this history, we stay entrapped by it and continue to act out its consequences. There is a lot of power in the simple act of bringing this into consciousness. Once I am aware of the reasons for certain actions and certain behaviors, I gain a freedom from them. I may then choose to continue these actions and behaviors or to work at changing them. But, for honesty's sake, I must emphasize that this change will require work and perhaps some hard work. Many of us have not been prepared to be reflective, to bring things into awareness, to allow ourselves to feel the pain of memories and feelings that will emerge, and then to remain with the process to allow it to achieve some healing. It is easier to get busy again, run away, or drown oneself in some distractions.

I am not a professional therapist. I hesitate to go into this topic of healing much more deeply. It is the people who have reacted with some relief and shared this sense of newly found freedom with me who prompt me to go on. It is also from my personal realization that, as a priest and a Christian, I share the call to be "ministers of reconciliation" (2 Cor. 5:18). Like any human being, I have been scarred and wounded by life. No one is exempt from this journey of the heart. Some are much more wounded than others. Some have to face deep wounds of childhood abuse, rejection, or betrayal. Others have experienced some similar traumas in their adult lives by going through a divorce, the loss of a child, or other terrible experiences. I do not make light of any of these wounds. But in the context of this book, I am focusing on the wounds resulting from some family and church dysfunctions. I am looking at the Irish experience in particular, for it is the one I know best. Others may see a parallel or similar experience in another ethnic setting. And the way to deal with these types of wounds may help in other personal healing processes as well. Let me share some reflections on the way to healing and reconciliation.[30]

Acknowledgment or Denial

In the previous chapters we surveyed the history of the Irish Catholic experience, especially among its émigrés in the New World. We have looked at history, not to gather the facts or be an expert in history, but to understand the reasons and causes for the effects that can still be discerned. The need for some self-dignity, the need for respectability before one's adversaries or oppressors (British or American), the pain of remembering what was left behind, the feelings of guilt and shame, an anger that could not be faced or channeled — all these were reasons for the suppression of old wounds. The scars, nonetheless, continued to be there and, at times, to fester again. It is only now, I have suggested, that the space of numerous years and decades allows many to look at the history and the causes with more objectivity.

So now the challenge is whether to acknowledge the old wounds or to deny them. They will not simply go away. One time, as I spoke to a group of interested listeners at an Irish festival, a psychiatric nurse who works in a nursing home commented that of all her patients, the Irish often seemed the most traumatized by long years of hurtful experiences. They exhibited this trauma by shying away from help, resisting human attempts to comfort and accompany them. The letter I quoted at the beginning of this chapter came from the pen of a woman in her late eighties who is now in a nursing facility in Canada. The truth set her free. Knowing and acknowledging the past breaks through a logjam of opinions, fantasies, and mistaken judgments. It also is the beginning of the healing of painful feelings that have resulted from the lack of awareness of the true past.

Besides the healing of the wounds of one's own painful experiences, the acknowledgment of our history and woundedness opens us up to a compassion for the painful experiences of others. In this compassion we find solidarity with other groups, and this too is a source of healing for our humanity. I felt this solidarity myself when I heard a panel at Boston University discuss the lingering scars of slavery among black Americans. Similar to the Irish experience of the famine, it is only now, one hundred and fifty years later, that African Americans are able to begin to look at the slavery experience and the residue of soul scarring that remains, especially among the young. "Slavery is not dead and done, and it won't be until we find the words to talk about it," said one commentator. The sense of poor self-worth, the tendency to turn to violence, and the propensity for suicide (all of these particularly strong especially among black adolescent males) were given as indications of such lingering trauma. I think that the profile of many adult men and women both among the Irish and among blacks would also show a remarkable resemblance. In the film *The Commitments*, the narrator, Jimmy, talks about how the Irish are the "blacks" of Europe. Another very interesting parallel is the rise in the number of African Americans who are returning to visit sites in Africa in order to understand their ancestors and what they left behind when they were brought to the New World. In revisiting the past, they come to know the present and themselves.

Still another corroboration of this need for healing that goes on, even after generations of change, comes from the Native American scene. When out in South Dakota a few years ago, I visited a Benedictine monastery that sits in the middle of the Dakota plains.[31] The monks have been there for some time and ministered to Native Americans in local reservations. They no longer have adequate numbers to personally minister to the people as they once did. But a center for Native Americans at the abbey continues to be important for them. This center has, as one of its purposes, the reconciliation of Native Americans, particularly the young, to a healthier place in the South Dakota landscape. Father Stan described the lingering effects of the oppression and displacement of Native Americans in the early years of the West that have manifested themselves in restlessness, alcoholism, violence, and suicide. It all sounded terribly familiar. Would that Irish Americans knew how much their history intersected with people such as African Americans and Native Americans. Our history, on various levels, is so much the same. We are not alone in our search for healing. And we can also be of help and support to each other. I am also, coincidentally, reminded that a large group of Native Americans reached out to the Irish during the famine to support them and send them food in their time of need.

How much easier it is, on the other hand, just to blame one's parents, one's teachers, priests and nuns, the church, the British, and whoever comes our way. This is a principal way of denial. Just blame someone else. This is particularly tempting to us today. We live in a litigious society. If something happens to us, some accident occurs, we want to sue someone immediately and be paid for our pain. Someone else must be blamed, must be guilty, and must pay. This is not a healthy way to live. It is much more difficult to really face our wounds, to name them and be clear about them. Indeed, perhaps someone is responsible for them. If that is the case, then that person has to be clearly identified, and no one else. I must also look at the hurts and identify them — how they have affected my sense of trust, my sense of justice, as well as my self-esteem and the ability to relate freely to those in my life, to those in authority, and to the world about me in general. I probably need to talk it out with someone and really get the story clear. And I need to pray for healing. This is the way to freedom, healing, and reconciliation.

Overcoming Guilt, Shame, and Self-Victimization

It is no wonder that some have chosen to deny or run from the pain of what has gone before them in their lives.

That avoidance doesn't really solve anything. Just as sad is the realization that the path for some people has been one of becoming mired in guilt, shame, or self-blame. This too is not the way to freedom or healing. Unfortunately, it can happen without one being aware of it and, as we have seen before, it is something that can be passed on from one generation to another.

The damage that can be done to a person, even unknowingly, was brought home to me on a visit to Northern Ireland. While in the city of Derry, we stopped at the Columba House of Prayer and Reconciliation.[32] Our group of pilgrims was treated to a talk about the work of the House by Alex Bradley, a psychologist on the staff. He spoke movingly of the work to bring Catholics and Protestants together to deal with their fears, angers, and the scars of old wounds. But what particularly struck me was Alex's incidental telling of his own story. He had grown up as a Catholic in a Protestant environment. He did not realize how much he had devalued himself until he went off to do some volunteer service work in Africa, where, with the help of others who appreciated him, he discovered himself and his own sense of self-worth. He returned to his native Derry, where, by reaching out in compassion in seeking the healing of others, he appears to have found healing for his own woundedness.

This experience of being hurt or devalued is not rare. Many women have felt devalued and experience the feeling of having no voice, whether in their homes, society, or the church. Abused children have tended to blame themselves and think of themselves as bad or dirty. Guilt and shame can be insidious forces in a person's life until they are brought into the light and better understood. In addition to many personal hurts and scars, I have indicated one that is prevalent among Irish Catholics. During the famine, many back in England, including those in high positions of church and state, preached that the Irish were

being punished for their own sins and that God's justice
should be allowed to take its course. Like children who
have been repeatedly told by their parents that they are no
good, many poor Irish believed this too. They submitted,
with passive resignation, to what they thought was God's
wrathful hand upon them. Priests and nuns imbibed this
message too and helped to pass it on to the people. A lot of
guilt, shame, and the spiritualizing away of pain has been
the heritage of the Irish. "Offer it up" was the solution
to everything. The real causes of the hurts, meanwhile,
were ignored and eventually forgotten. A melancholy sadness, however, kept the memory alive on one level, and a
suppressed anger always awaited awakening.

Jerry wrote to me from Australia to say,

> I have just finished reading your book for the first
> time. There will be others. I am an Australian of
> Scots/Irish descent. I was brought up in an English
> outpost where our Celtic heritage was never men-
> tioned as we were taught that the English were world
> leaders and the Catholics were dreadful in the fullest
> sense of the word. I became a Catholic anyway, as
> were all my original ancestors and two of my grand-
> parents. But it is not complete. I need to delve deeper
> and find more. . . . I do not know enough about Vati-
> can Two and where it leads us. I need to know. I will
> find out.

Jerry has chosen the way to healing and wholeness. He
has resonated with the Celtic story and found a sense of
personal dignity in this story. He is willing to do some
work to find out more of the past, and about the church,
in order to understand himself.

We all need to make sense of our lives. We all need to
find meaning. It is the healthy way to bring the causes
of our pains and wounds into awareness and face them.
It is healthier to let our feelings of anger emerge and be

focused on the responsible people and the underlying reasons. Feeling angry is not a sin, and the avoidance of anger has imprisoned many people. Feeling helpless, victimized, and wallowing in self-pity are one side to such avoidance. Bitterness, constant criticism, engaging in forms of racism or sexism, and looking down on others are other expressions of the walking wounded.

God wants us to be whole, as God wants us to be holy. God wants us to be happy, even if we must deal with certain inevitable pains and problems in life. We are not, however, to manufacture sufferings for ourselves or continue to carry them on from one generation to another. A path to forgiveness, of letting go of the past, of opening new options for the future, of enjoying a state of reconciliation with oneself, with one's people and family, with one's ancestors, and with one's God — these are all possible for those who would take on the task of healing. I need to learn from the past and let it go. I need to accept the good things from the past and reject the hurtful. I cannot be ashamed of who I am. Let me say proudly, "I am glad to be me. I am glad to be an Irish American. I am glad to be an Irish Catholic." I am not better than anyone else who is different, but I can be happy to be myself. Drawing on my deeper Celtic and Christian roots has brought me, as well as many others, to a better understanding and acceptance of my place in the church and the world of today.

Gillian is a woman from Wales who shared these thoughts with me:

> I finished reading your book just five minutes ago and, combined with a feeling of warmth and appreciation, was an ecstatic YES, YES, YES — so much of what you say and the spirit in which you say it is so very close to my own spirit. My own background is of an angry breakaway Christian, a feminist, in-

volved for it seems like a lifetime, in peace issues and women's issues, searching all the way to make sense of the violence and control all around and being close to the land in the rural part of Wales.

I do not know where Gillian's search will lead her. But in beginning to deal with her anger and focus it more clearly, and in thus sorting out the good from the bad in her understanding of the past, she is certainly on a path of healing and reconciliation.

Reconciliation with the Church

For some Irish Catholics, one of the most difficult issues today is dealing with their anger with the Catholic Church. Among all the immigrant groups to come from Europe to the New World in the nineteenth century, the Irish were the least anticlerical. Today, especially in Ireland itself, there is a good deal of anticlericalism and anger with the "priest-ridden Church."[33] Irish Americans are not usually so outspoken about their anger but may be more apathetic when they become disillusioned with the church of their ancestors. For many, there are many mixed feelings about their continuing to be Catholics. Some have been personally hurt by priests and nuns and carry those scars around. Some have simply become angry at what they perceive as hypocritical, authoritarian, or controlling behavior on the part of church leaders.

Everyone's story is unique and each person has to be responsible for his or her own life's story. I hope, however, that any reader can perceive that spiritual journey and spiritual growth necessitate dealing with whatever is in our lives. Where your journey will take you, as in Gillian's story above, cannot be predicted, and I do not feel that it has to go in one particular direction. For those on the journey I have the following thoughts to consider in making the journey of reconciliation with the church and with one's Christian background.

First, I think that many Catholics have to reconsider, and perhaps readjust, the meaning of the church in their lives. After the Reformation in the sixteenth century, Protestants tended to deify the Bible and often treated the sacred Scriptures in a very literal and fundamentalist fashion. Catholics tended to do the same with the church. A passive and uneducated Catholic laity simply depended on the church, as represented by its leaders, to tell them the law of God and what was good and bad in their lives. I am afraid we lost the sense of the human in the church. That is very easy to do. Even today many Catholics, and other Christians and other believers, look for a religion that is certain in its giving of definitive answers, full of miracles, apparitions, and offering clear evidence of the working of the divine. The same dynamic took place in the time of Jesus. People pressed Jesus for signs, healings, cures, and miracles. They often could not hear his message for their intent on the miraculous. His own humanity, which eventually led to his passion and death, was not comprehensible to them. In fact, the humanity of Jesus has been scandalous for many who prefer to believe in a divine and miraculous Jesus only.

The humanity of the church has suffered the same reaction. We have often had difficulty with accepting our own humanity, as well as the humanity of popes, bishops, and priests. We all are human, fallible, sinful creatures. In my own early years as a priest I became aware that people often put me on a pedestal, a very scary place to be. The need to be perfect, implied in this vocation for so many of us, is a terrible burden to put on anyone (or to place on oneself), and no human being can achieve it. So, accepting the humanity of the church is a first corrective in our awareness of the church and our attempts to reconcile ourselves with its sinfulness. And this may mean, after dealing with anger and hurts, to forgive someone who has caused us pain in our relationship to the church.

The second observation I would make flows from this humanity of the church and its ministers. All that I have been saying in this book about the need for healing, for a new consciousness, for letting go of the past, for a new look at the healthier part of our Christian story applies also, and maybe especially, to priests and nuns. So many of the clergy, brought up in the Irish Catholic mold described earlier, are in need of healing. They need to adjust their own spiritual perspective of the world, people, love, sexuality, and embodiment. The education they received in the past did not prepare them to live in this new, post–Vatican II age, this postmodern era, this pluralistic society in which we live. The new church, which is yet to emerge, is now in a time of transition. The place of the clergy in this church has to change. There needs to be more collaboration with the laity, both men and women, and recognition of the gifts that all of us, in our diversity, bring to the unity of the church. Some, both clergy and laity, are finding this transition very painful and tend to want to retreat to older, firmer structures where the identity of priest, nun, and layperson was much more clear cut. I wish the present time wasn't so painful. It requires a lot of patience, tolerance, courage, and trust for us to move with the church. And, as we have to forgive some clerical figures in our life, we may also have to help them find their own healing.

Marian Woodman, a Jungian psychologist, gave me a good insight into our present dilemma. In a lecture, she was commenting on the Jungian theme of the paradoxical nature of the unity of opposites. What happens when you have two values or two perspectives that seem to be opposed to each other? The tendency is always to choose one and drop the other. Woodman claimed that the more creative thing to do is to hold the opposites in tension with each other. She illustrated this by holding out her arms and picturing herself as holding an opposite good in each hand. She then brought attention to the pose, one of crucifixion, as she held out her arms and became tired. Her point was that, by holding two opposites in tension, and in pain, a new, third reality will be born. I think that is what is happening in the church. On the one hand, many people treasure the heritage of the church — Jesus, Mary, and the saints; the sacraments, with their wonderful ritual and symbolic meaning for human living; the sense of community and being God's people; the treasures of social teachings on the meaning of life, science, and war and peace; the openness to the Trinity and the mystery of God; the whole mystical tradition and the prayer heritage of the ages; great educational, medical, cultural, and scientific commitments; and the positive accomplishments of pope, bishops, and institutional church proclaiming values to a confused world. There is a lot there to hold on to. But on the other hand, some feel the pain of being women, gay people, or others being devalued in an authoritarian church that does not understand and appreciate such values as love and sexuality. They often feel underestimated and unappreciated in the ways that they, as laypeople, both married and single, bring their gifts to the spreading of Jesus' gospel today. These two opposites can be difficult to keep in creative tension. Only by trusting in God's creative action, through the power of the Wild Goose, will new life and meaning emerge. The question each of us has to answer is, "Is this effort worthwhile, and am I willing to travel a long, painful journey?" How much pain can I tolerate, how much patience and hope can I gather up for my own journey, how much energy am I willing to invest in the Christian enterprise?

As an American, I instinctively share the repulsion of any authority that tries to take away my freedom. I do not always like the authoritarian and controlling ways that church authorities employ. I wish they would be better at communicating with and respecting others. Condemnations usually do more harm than good. I am, however, becoming increasingly aware of how much more insidious is the way that our American culture, through consumerism, the media, and advertising, tries to manipulate and control me. It plays on my self-image and my sense of self-worth and self-esteem. I can easily become a slave to fashion, to having the "right kind" of clothes, fragrances, automobile, and so forth. We are not nearly as free as we think we are. In this context, I believe that the church is one of the few voices that speak out for true human dignity, for the value of all people (even when it doesn't always live out these values itself). Of course, I also believe that the church is the body of Christ, the suffering, very human, scarred body of Christ, and is not our own invention. It is the same church for which some of my Irish ancestors probably suffered because of fidelity to their faith in Christ.

I am convinced that I can deal with a lot of uncertainty and change and imperfection if I have some vision of hope. This vision, in part at least, comes from an awareness of the rich tradition of our past, which continues to live and bear fruit. A renewed worldview, a new awareness and consciousness, may be needed to sustain this hope and this vision. It is in looking at the rich tradition of the church in the first millennium that I have found the fertile soil or ground of such a tradition. Looking back to that time before all the splits and defensiveness of the second millennium, I believe we can find food for our soul in the Christian spirituality of times closer to the beginnings. The Second Vatican Council asked us to go back to our roots, to come to know the Bible anew and understand Jesus and the early church in its sources. The history of the early church, a small and infant church that took roots in an alien and pagan society, can teach us much

about how we are to live in this new, postmodern pluralistic world. Traditions, such as the Benedictine monastic
vision, are helpful in bringing new life to our vision. For
Irish Catholics, and for many other Christians as well, reclaiming the insights of the Celtic Christian tradition can
be helpful both in the healing of wounds and in the finding of the new vision needed for the third millennium. The
final chapters of this book turn to some positive aspects
of this Celtic tradition that might guide us in our spiritual
awakening.

Chapter Six

Finding One's Celtic Spiritual Roots (1)

Imagination and Story

*F*OLLOWING ONE OF MY WORKSHOPS on Celtic spirituality, a young married man, John, surprised and delighted me with a poem he wrote. He calls it "Things Celtic," and I share it with you here.

> Recently — and by surprise —
> I love the things Celtic —
> Not the leprechaun,
> not the smiling eyes,
> not the pint of stout,
> but things of a deeper green,
> things of druidic mystery,
> things of Celtic circularity,
> things as round and hard
> as the Celtic cross.
>
> I will laugh at the leprechaun,
> clasp arms around my friends
> and sing the pub song
> and taste the woodiness of the pint.
>
> But give me room to howl with
> the mystical wild men of my past.
> And when I die, weep not with beads,

> bury me not in a grave — rather — plant
> me in the place of my resurrection.[34]

This poem is light and whimsical, and yet it expresses some deep sentiments. I believe that John has captured the spirit of the Celts, and especially the spirituality of the Celtic Christian. I would like to take a look at some aspects of that spirituality in this chapter. First, I will have to tell you what I mean by "spirituality."

A Way to View the World

The word "spirituality" may scare some people off. It sounds so otherworldly. A large number of people probably think of the spiritual as something apart from this world. And that certainly is one type of spirituality. But spirituality also has to do with how we see and comprehend the basic realities of human existence — realities such as life, relationships, and our purpose for living. It is concerned with how we make meaning of and understand our time here on earth, as well as our view of that which transcends our world and what we comprehend as the divine or supernatural. So I like to think of my own spirituality as my particular worldview — my basic view of all reality and how I fit everything into it, including (and maybe, especially) that which is most profound and meaningful in my life.

We have taken a look at nineteenth-century Irish and Irish American spirituality. In so doing, we should be able to imagine what was the religious worldview of those times. God was thought to be above and beyond this world, often pictured essentially as policeman and judge. Jesus was both divine and human, a person who brought God closer to us in a loving way but also someone to adore and keep at a distance. Michelangelo's Sistine Chapel mural of Jesus at the last judgment images the

Christ as divine judge. In this belief system, Mary and the saints are all much closer to us than is God. In this portrait, our life itself is a trial. We are very prone to sin, especially in the area of how we use our sexuality. The church is there to guide us and tell us what God wants of us. We must be faithful to attending Sunday Mass regularly. We must go to confession often to gain forgiveness for our lapses and regain the state of grace and our union with God so we will be ready to die in the state of grace. Grace is imaged almost as a material commodity that is acquired by attendance at Mass (which the priest does on our behalf), by reception of the other sacraments, and through practices such as novenas, First Fridays, and abstinence from meat on Fridays. These are all important ways to keep our souls clean and ready to die. The world is a place full of temptations and much evil. In fact, some adherents to this spirituality may consider that which is secular and profane to be basically evil. This might include material reality itself, including the human body and sexuality. Only the soul is important. "Give me souls; take everything else," Saint John Bosco was fond of saying. It seems that the creedal affirmation of our belief in the "resurrection of the body" was overlooked in lieu of "saving one's soul."

How different from this is the spirituality of our Celtic ancestors. We will look at various particular aspects of this spirituality in the next couple of chapters. But in general, I see its primary importance is that it breaks through these false divisions and so-called dualisms. Heaven and earth are intimately close. All creation, all material reality is holy. The ordinary events and things of daily life are graced with the presence of God. The earth is holy. My body and my sexuality are holy. Incidentally, one of the realizations I have had in rediscovering this type of spirituality is that it is not only closer to the first millennium of Christians but it also resonates with our Jewish roots. There seem to be a lot of similarities between Celtic spirituality and Jewish spirituality. First, they both understand a day as beginning with sunset. This is a profound insight, expressed in the belief that darkness comes first and light emerges from darkness. Winter begins the new year (on November 1) and spring emerges from it. But there are other similarities as well. The holiness of the everyday and the ordinary are to be found in both traditions, as are the place of beauty and sensuality and the importance of sharpening the senses to behold beauty and goodness by slowing down in prayer or, for the Jew, the *Shabbat*. Hospitality is a value in both traditions as well. Finally, I see that curiosity and the desire to understand, to study, and to learn are common to both. My finding the closeness of these two traditions is another link for me for uniting us as Christians to the wider human search for the transcendent and to another great religious tradition, in this case the Jewish one.[35]

In our Judeo-Christian traditions, God, it is true, is a God far above and beyond us but is basically a good and loving Creator. As Christians we further believe that this God has come close to us in the Word and the Spirit. Jesus, the Word of God, lives among us through the resurrection. To find ourselves joined to Christ's journey through life and death is our Christian vocation. In this vocation, Mary and the saints, as well as all our ancestors, accompany and aid us. And we are called to be concerned, not just with the morality of our sexuality, but with our relationships in a much wider sense — for the welfare of my friends, family, communities, town, and country, the justice needs of all peoples, and for the very earth and material creation itself. This certainly is a different way to see reality.

I am a Benedictine monk. I follow, as rule of life, the way laid out by Saint Benedict (480–547). It is a way of community, of the importance of all the small acts of

everyday living, of praising God in liturgy, of knowing
God in the Scriptures and praising God daily, particularly
in the psalms of the Hebrew Scriptures. I have, happily,
found this spirituality to be free of many of the divisions
and dualisms I have mentioned above. The way of the
Celts, also one that goes back to the middle of the first
millennium, has therefore enlivened my Benedictine spirituality with some particular gifts. When I am asked how
Celtic spirituality has aided me personally and what it
has added to my Benedictine monastic tradition, I tend to
think of two aspects of my spiritual life. The first has to
do with the importance of the imagination. The second
has to do with the importance of story.

The Religious Imagination

Studying the Celtic Christian experience has heightened
my awareness of the importance of the imagination. So
much of our religion, and often our spirituality too, is
merely in the head — mostly ideas, thoughts, concepts.
We confuse doctrines, creeds, and beliefs, as well as rules
and morals, with spirituality. Now I certainly do think
that doctrine and morality are important. As a Christian I
believe in the absolute importance of doctrines such as the
Trinity, the incarnation, the sacraments, the communion
of saints. And I believe not only in the Ten Command-
ments but also in the Sermon on the Mount for indicating
a moral way of life demanded by Christ of those who
would be his disciples. But spirituality is, as indicated
above, how we integrate all of this in our view of the
world, and in how we live out these doctrines and rules,
how we live with them day by day.

It is our imagination that is crucial here. How we imagine something will motivate us and guide us. If we want
to change how we think of something, the best way is to
change how we imagine it. If I imagine heaven as some-

thing far away and far beyond me, then I will act in one way as I go through my mundane acts of daily living. But if I imagine God and heaven as being warp and woof of human life here and now, I need to live differently.

The Celts were an extremely imaginative people. Just look at their art. The spiral and the circle appear consistently in the art of the Celts, both pagan and Christian. That tells us something about their view of reality, the manner in which they saw everything. Things had no beginning or end. There was a sense of the eternal in the here and now. This is a way of perceiving reality that is comfortable with paradox, with gray areas of life. Black and white divisions, such as this life and the next life, the sacred and the secular, male and female, the body and soul, and many other dualisms of realities, give way to a "both/and" way of seeing things versus an "either/or" approach to reality. Life is both more simple and more complex in this way of seeing things. I need to live with a sense of mystery and accept that I cannot figure everything out. I cannot comprehend God even though I know God is intimately present in all I do, in all I touch, in all of history, and in all of the events of the world about me. This is a mystical view of reality. All is not quite what it seems to be but yet is more than it seems to be. The scientific knowledge of reality is only one way of seeing things. The way of the heart and the spirit sees another, equally real, dimension. The imagination opens up a bigger world for us with greater possibilities of what it means to be human.

There are many things our imaginations can learn from our Celtic ancestors. The Celts were a colorful people. In the first century, Roman writers described their brightly colorful clothes and remarked on how well groomed they were. They were visually alive! The human spirit needs to express itself in matter. The spirit needs to be nourished by good art, the beauty of the environment, and know itself to be connected to the beauty of all of creation. These things both feed the spirit and express its very nature. I have always been struck by a saying of Dorothy Day, that wonderful woman who worked among the poor in the Bowery of New York. She loved to repeat a quotation from Dostoyevski's novel *The Idiot*, which says that only beauty will save the world. Beauty is not a luxury. Good art, music, and literature are basic to the human spirit. Feeding ourselves with the inanities of much of television and the public media of today is destructive to the human spirit.

The Celts were a highly verbal people, belonging to an oral culture in which bards and poets were respected and were envied because of the influence that they exerted in their society. I have come to realize how important poetry, song, and stories are in the spiritual life. Our awareness of God, our praise and thanksgiving of God and the gifts of God, and even our awareness of how we sin by not cooperating with the God of creation are all honed by the music we listen to, the books we read, the movies and plays we watch, and the way we socialize and entertain ourselves. None of this is separate from the life of the Spirit and, truly, all is part of it.

The Celts had a sense of space and time that went beyond our scientific ways of measurement. *Thin places* and *thin times* were those areas where the ordinary veil that separated this world and the other tended to break down and even disappear. Liminal areas such as mountaintops, the incoming tide of the ocean, isolated islands, wells that bridged the inner and outer earth, as well as those places made holy by the lives of holy people — all these were considered to be thin places. Many old, sacred places in Ireland, such as the ruins of early Celtic monasteries, are now covered over with tombstones. People wanted to be buried in such holy places, thin places, the "place of their resurrection," as the Celts were wont to call it and to which John alluded to in his poem quoted above.

Thin times, on the other hand, were times such as the great yearly feasts. The pagan Celtic new year feast of *Samhain,* celebrated around November 1, with its veneration of the dead, became All Saints Day and All Souls Day in the Christian calendar. *Imbolc,* on February 1, was incorporated in the feast of Saint Brigid. *Beltaine,* on May 1, became part of the Easter and spring festivals. *Lughnasa,* on August 1, was the forerunner of the annual pilgrimage up to Patrick's holy mountain of Croagh Patrick, and this festival also became the occasion of the many local village agricultural fairs. And, of course, the Irish wake is a prime example of a thin time. Here, in the presence of the corpse of the deceased, one waited for the soul to depart, something that might take three days to happen. While people waited, never leaving the body alone, they helped the soul to depart with song, dance, food, and a few drinks as well.

This sense of imagination that so pervaded the Celtic view of the world and of the divine as well has influenced my own spirituality. "Care of the soul," as Thomas Moore uses this phrase in his writings and talks, means tending to the moist areas of our human life in reading, writing, singing, and tending to the senses and emotions.[36] These "soul-full" things nourish the spirit. I believe that giving more heed to these things has aided my own spiritual life. I certainly have a much greater appreciation of poetry than I formerly did. Praying the psalms, the great poetry of the Bible, feeds the spiritual imagination. I do that with much greater relish and appreciation now. Good liturgy, ritual, and ceremony are a great part of our Catholic heritage, and I glory in their value and importance. The Scriptures in my daily life, as well as other good reading, are crucial too. And not only does this influence my personal spiritual life but it also affects how I preach and share my faith. Yes, the religious imagination is important to recover, and the Celts can help us to do that.

My Story — Our Story

I now turn to a second way in which Celtic spirituality has made a difference in my own spiritual search. It has to do with the importance of story. The Celtic tradition has been largely an oral one, where the spoken word carried great weight and dignity. I have already alluded to the importance of bards and poets. Another person highly respected in the Celtic tradition is the *seanchaí,* or storyteller, and this person's role has continued in importance even in the era of the written word. Everybody loves a story. The best sermons are those that tell a story. From the Celts we can also learn how important story is for our spiritual journey.

At the time of the Irish rebellion in 1916, remembered as the Easter Rising, a poet by the name of Patrick Pearse was one of the main protagonists. He drew upon two figures for his inspiration. One was the old Irish hero, Cúchulain, the central character in the Ulster Cycle of the Red Branch Warriors. The other figure is the Christ — suffering, dying, and rising. The mythology of these two heroes inspired Pearse and others. And in many ways, each hero was shadowed in the other. Cúchulain died while tied to a tree, fighting his last great battle. Isn't that a figure of the Christ? And Christ was so easily accepted by the Celts in their conversion to Christianity because he was the hero who suffered and died for them in the way of their Celtic forebears. The faith dimension came in the belief in the resurrection. But it was all of a piece. The story is one. In the Christian era, monks replaced druids and bards. The great stories of the Bible embraced the old heroic tales without completely replacing them.

The Celts have strongly reinforced in me the conviction that there is a "Big Story" of which we are all a part. Abraham and Sarah, Ruth and David, Isaiah and Judith, Jesus and Mary, Benedict and Scholastica, Patrick and Brigid are all in this "Big Story." The Celtic vision saw them all as still alive and moving and living with the people. The Celtic sense of time allowed them to believe that someone like Brigid, for example, could have been present as midwife to Mary at the birth of Jesus. Scientific, historical facts were secondary to the deeper truths of humanity expressed in a mythological manner. We are all part of the one story and we are all interconnected. In our own time, in this age of story of space travel and going back in time or ahead in time, is this so fanciful as we once would have believed?

As Christians we gather at the Eucharist, where the liturgy of the Word has assumed a much more significant role since the Second Vatican Council. The significance of story has been returned to us as the Bible has been made more readily available to all. We gather as one people, God's people, to hear God's Word, our story, and reflect on its meaning for today. Nowhere is this more striking than at the Easter Vigil, the central liturgical event of the year (the Christian Easter Rising), when we gather in the darkness to hear the stories of creation, of the call and journey of Abraham, of the liberation of the Hebrews from Egypt under Moses, and the other stories that climax in the story of the resurrection of Christ from the dead. There is continuity, there is a purpose, there is a development, there is movement. The Christian story is a spiral and not just the cyclical return to the same place, as was the understanding of time in the pagan religions before Christianity.

All of this is not just our story. It is also my story. This may, perhaps, be a revolutionary insight for us contemporary people of the West. Why do I say it is revolutionary? I believe it is so because we have become such individualized and privatized people. The divorce of the Bible from the Catholic faithful in the post-Tridentine years of the sixteenth to the twentieth centuries has left many without a sense of the bigger story. We have accepted the broken-up story of the civil culture and are drowning in our own loneliness and in our sense of isolation. Our private freedoms are so important that we shy away from community and commitments. How difficult it is, for instance, for young people to commit themselves to a relationship or a vocation today. I don't think it is because most of them are bad or selfish. Without the support of the community and commonly shared values, the burden on a person to give of himself or herself fully is enormous and almost impossible. With the disappearance of the extended family and its traditions, and the isolationism in society at large, two people giving themselves to each other in marriage, for instance, have to live that commitment completely by themselves, depending on the ability to love each other no matter what. It is too often too much to bear alone. Unless their story is part of Christ's story, their lives part of living the gospel and relying on God's grace to be faithful, they are expecting too much.

We live in a very psychological age, and our pervasive need to get help for our inner life is probably connected to our individualism. The common myths, values, and beliefs of tribes once gave people their identity. Now people must search for that identity, sometimes endlessly through their entire life span. And for all the technological availability of information, so many have few close friends, certainly few of the type with whom to share their personal and intimate lives. Countless numbers must turn to professional counselors ("paid friends," as they are sometimes called) to have someone to share their lives. This "Lone Ranger" type of existence is, again, quite a burden for an individual to bear on one's own.

On the other hand, what if I find that I have a story,

and that my story connects with a bigger story? For a people raised on television that comes as a shock. When we watch television, a story is broken up into small segments, interrupted by commercials, neatly concluded in thirty minutes. And if we don't like the story, we just change the channel. It is easy to think my life is like that — just a number of disassociated incidents and happenings, something I should be able to easily change if I do not like it. But to begin to see continuity in my entire life story, a common thread going through ups and downs, joys and sorrows, and my successes and failures as well, opens up another view of life. To see my story as connected with the stories of others, both living and dead, might change how I see my life. That is how the Celtic Christians saw their lives.

Could it be that our ancestors, including but not restricted to the Celts, had a greater grasp of life's meaning than we do? Surprisingly enough, there is much in modern science that indicates they did. Jungian psychology tells us that we all carry around within us the common archetypes, images of reality, that surpass our private experience. The meaning of human realities such as love, heroism, journey, and the images of king or queen, warrior, lover, and wise shaman[37] are archetypal to all people. The stories and myths of worldwide cultures confirm a common base of human understandings. We seem to be hardwired in our humanity when it comes to basic feelings, instincts, and ways of understanding ourselves.

Another interesting clue to our common story comes from other sources. Saint Augustine, in the fourth century, wrote of his inner search as touching memories of what had gone before. Science today proclaims that life is a web of interdependent relationships. Modern physics sees life and consciousness as an unfolding of the totality of what was contained in the initial explosion of matter. All that has been since the beginning of the universe is to be found within each one of us. The past still lives within us. And we know now that each of our bodies is composed of the same matter as the stars. Truly, all is one. But do we feel that or are we conscious of that unity?

It is important to get in touch with my own story, to begin to see my life story as a whole and as a continuous, ongoing story. God has been working through it all, day by day, though not always very clearly. I am part of a bigger story too as I build on the inheritance of my ancestors and prepare the world for my heirs. The Celtic sense of community, of tribe, and of an awareness of being close to the other world all feed my imagination in this regard. I have already mentioned, for instance, that I was named after my two grandfathers. I have been delighted to learn that it is the belief among some primitive peoples that you have the spirit of your grandparents, who look after you. I am convinced that my grandfathers still bless me and mentor me. They are with me, as are my parents and other ancestors, as well as all the angels and saints, especially Jesus and Mary. I do not walk alone in my journey. My story is part of a bigger story.

That conviction alone is not sufficient to put me at ease with my own story and tell it openly. That takes time, prayer, and reflection. As we go through life, we are only too aware of the mistakes we make, the failures and betrayals we encounter, the wrong decisions made at times. Coming to peace with all that has been my story takes time and requires a sense of freedom from fear and shame, a knowledge that all has been part of the one story. I know that my life has had its failures. I have not always been the loving and compassionate person I wish to be. I have made decisions that I would change if I could go back and do it again. But accepting myself as I am, here and now, is accepting my part in the story. People love me as I am, despite all that has been. This has helped me to realize that God, too, loves me for who I am, probably much more so as the One who knows what is deep in my heart.

Tradition, Culture, and Experience

A retreat master once told us that a healthy spirituality must have a balance of three ingredients. The first is tradition, that which is handed down to us. For us Christians that means the Scriptures, the church of saints and sinners, and a sacramental way of viewing and celebrating reality as graced by God. In brief, it is the Christ story that has endured for two thousand years. The second ingredient is culture, as we relate our tradition to our own times. We must understand the times in which we live and the history that has brought it about. The third ingredient is experience, which mediates between tradition and culture. It is the area by which I become personally involved in my tradition and live in my own culture. I think that this way of looking at things agrees with the Celtic vision, the Celtic Christian worldview that we have been investigating. In addition, perhaps, the Celtic vision is also one that stresses the imagination in relating to our tradition, culture, and experience. The Celtic inheritance helps us to see and hear our spirituality with eyes and ears that can image our religious tradition in soulful and life-giving ways.

Chapter Seven

Finding One's
Celtic Spiritual Roots (2)
Images of God, Humanity,
and the Universe

A NUMBER OF PEOPLE TODAY seek a more mystical or contemplative type of spirituality. But I do wonder if the words "mystical" and "contemplative" might scare others off. Such people do not want an otherworldly or dreamy kind of spirituality. In the Celtic tradition, and other older spiritualities as well, a mystical view is not such an ethereal or otherworldly view at all. It is quite down to earth. I understand a mystical view as one that sees behind the veil of ordinary darkness that separates this world and the other, between heaven and earth. The mystic is one who is very aware of the intimate presence of God in everything. I think that this is what the famous Jesuit theologian Karl Rahner was talking about some twenty-five years ago when he predicted that the ordinary Christian of the future would be a mystic or not a Christian at all. Paula, an Irish friend of mine, is one such contemporary mystic. She wrote to me once in this way:

It is amazing to be in the middle of a crowded swilling bar in Boston engaged in conversation and be jolted abruptly by the spark of God's presence. A

few weeks ago I was at the opening of a new bar in
Cambridge; a friend from Ireland is co-owner. The
place was saturated with individuals and the life was
fairly eeking out the front door. I was struck by the
realization of how much I miss the physical presence
of Jesus Christ. I mean to actually have seen the con-
tours of His face among so many faces. To gaze upon
the features and stand in His presence. What a healing that would be. I miss Him as I would miss a soul
mate from home.[38]

This letter confirms my belief that an Irish pub is often a
center of spirituality! Paula's mystical sense of God's presence, however, is not usually so conscious and manifest in
everyday life. The person who is a mystic apprehends the
divine on a certain level of his or her awareness without
necessarily having to think about it. This is what I meant
about the importance of the imagination in the last chapter. It is how we imagine things that often determines just
how aware we are of the presence of the divine in life. Let
us briefly consider what the Celtic sense of imagination
might offer to our awareness of who God is, who we are
as human beings, and what the universe in which we are
situated is all about.

Images of God

From a Christian point of view, I believe that the most
significant thing we can learn from Celtic Christianity
about God is the emphasis on the Three-in-One God. Yes,
I know that we Christians all believe in it, profess it in the
Creed, and know it is essential to Christianity. But how
this belief affects us in practice is another matter. A number of theologians believe that we, in the churches of the
West, have overemphasized the Christ, and the divinity of
Christ in particular, and only given lip service to the sig-

nificance of Father and Holy Spirit. Believers often pray to Christ as God and then rely on Mary and the saints, as human intermediaries, to be intercessors for them with the Christ.

The Celts took to Christianity quickly in the fifth and sixth centuries. They embraced the Three-in-One God, as they already had a vision of reality that saw life in triads. The Celtic Christians lived and breathed the Trinity. Everything had to be done in the name of the Triune God. When milking a cow, for example, the first three squirts of milk were to be splashed on the ground in the name of the Trinity. Celtic prayers are infused with the holy Three-in-One. Here is one of my favorite prayers from the collection called the *Carmina Gadelica,* a book of prayers and poems collected in the late-nineteenth century in the Scottish highlands by Alexander Carmichael from people who still lived a vibrant, oral, Celtic tradition:

> I lie down this night with God,
> And God will lie down with me;
> I lie down this night with Christ,
> And Christ will lie down with me;
> I lie down this night with the Spirit,
> And the Spirit will lie down with me;
> God and Christ and the Spirit
> Be lying down with me.[39]

I love this prayer because God is so intimate and close to me in it. The Celts had thousands of such prayers in which the Three-in-One God was close to them in all they did every day.

One legend has it that Saint Patrick used the three-leafed shamrock to teach about the Trinity. I myself like the Celtic image of the sun to help image the Triune God. In this image, God, the first person of the Trinity (called "the Father" in our tradition), is the sun itself. The Word, Christ, is the sunray that goes from the sun and touches us. God the Holy Spirit is the warmth and energy that the sun produces within us. Keep this image in mind as I reflect on the threefold way that God is in the very divine essence, and how God is for us.[40]

God the Father, simply referred to as "God" by Jesus and much of the scriptural tradition, is like the sun itself. This God cannot be directly looked upon or comprehended. The mass and volume and heat and size and power of the sun are beyond my experience to accurately imagine. And so is God. I think that this is an important aspect of God for us to have, and maybe to recover. I know some people who have walked away from God and church when life becomes too difficult or burdensome. God has let them down. But it is perhaps their own inadequate image of God that has failed them. So many of us do not have a sense of God that allows for mystery, that calls us to take off our shoes in the divine presence, that calls for a spirit of awe, wonder, and maybe even fear at times. We have reacted against our old images of God as judge, policeman, and vindictive leader, and reduced our God, at times, to a benevolent old grandfather. But when this image fails us in life's experiences, what do we have? A loss of the sense of transcendence, of "otherness," of "the holy" seems to be much the vogue today. Young people in particular grow up in a world devoid of that which is beyond us. Science and technology beguile us with the feeling of mastery and control, and this appears to eliminate the need for God.

God, first person of the Trinity, is, in this understanding, an immense abyss of being that embraces, and yet is much more than, this immense cosmos of which we are becoming more aware. When we come before this God to pray in thanksgiving and adoration, as we do at Mass, we need a sense of reverence and respect for mystery. I believe that one of the unforeseen and undesirable results of the post–Vatican Council liturgy, in our refinding of the importance of community at prayer, is an overemphasis at times on comforting and warm feelings of togetherness. These are legitimate needs and were formerly neglected. But an imbalance has at times resulted, to the detriment of the sense of the mysterious and awesome God before whom we gather to worship, though it is certainly as community and certainly as a people that we must see the divine image. We cannot look this God directly in the face and live. I find that the immensity of the created cosmos, of which we are just beginning to glimpse the depths and the beauty in the photos received from outer space, helps me to get some sense of the infinity and eternity of which this God breathes. This God cannot be trivialized into "the man upstairs" or made to conform to any human or created images.

This is God and we are not. The image of God, first person of the Trinity, is reassuring to us inasmuch as we concede that there is a power much beyond what we can understand. We can live with some mystery in our life and not expect to find the answer to everything. But of course, this image is also somewhat scary. Here our Christian faith tells us that God is Holy Spirit, intimately and imminently dwelling within us. In the sun image, this is the warmth and energy we feel from the sun. But certainly, no image or metaphor says it all. The Sequence of the Mass on Pentecost describes the Holy Spirit in wide terms and images such as our heart's unfailing light, the wisest and best of consolers, the soul's most welcome guest, sweet refreshment, and sweet repose. It goes on to further describe the presence of this Spirit as rest in labor, pleasant coolness in heat, consolation in woes, restorer of wounded souls, the one who bends stubborn hearts and wills, melts the frozen and warms the cold, and guides the wayward home.[41] All these are images of a mysterious, but very close God. We are never alone. The purpose of much of our spiritual life is to be transformed, so that our own inner self is in perfect harmony with this Spirit so that we move and live as one. This is the work of transformation that comes about by our losing ourselves in love, compassion, and asceticism, so that the God at our center emerges as our true self. The Celtic Christians felt the presence of this inner fire and recognized it in the image of the Wild Goose. This is a wonderful image that expresses the wildness, unpredictability, and passion of our God. God is so close to us and comforting to us. Yet, at the same time, this God pushes us into the unknown, sometimes beyond our limits, into the heart of the Triune Godhead itself. This Spirit-God is exhilarating but at times perhaps a bit frightening as well.

This perspective of God, while sometimes comforting and close, can also remain somewhat illusive and ethereal for us. And so we have the sunray, the Word spoken by the Father from all eternity, the Christ made flesh, the human face of God. If the Celts took to the Three-in-One God so quickly, they surely found their entrance into the mystery, as we must also, through the humanity of Jesus Christ. It is Jesus Christ, the second person of the Trinity, who is our access to the God who is transcendent and so far beyond us and also to the God who is within us. It is the Christ who makes known that this awesome, transcendent God is in fact a very benevolent God, one that we may even call *Abba,* a word that is more like "daddy." Jesus is the way to this God, as well as being our truth and life. And Jesus remains with us in the written word of the Scriptures, in the symbolic words of the sacraments, in the living words of the church community — all made accessible to us because of the indwelling of the Holy Spirit.

This human being, Jesus, was a God whom the Celts accepted and loved because he was like them and suffered with them, one who knew them from within. Here, over the centuries of oppression and pain, the Irish found meaning by their own living of the paschal mystery, the death and rising of their great hero, their high king, their sweet savior, their brother, Jesus Christ. The Celts, as lovers of stories, also embraced the Bible and came to know Jesus Christ as "the way, the truth, and the life" by coming to know the Gospels. They looked on Christ in the agony in the garden and on the cross, but also saw that his loving confidence in his *Abba* did not bring him relief or rescue. Suffering somehow must be a part of the human story. But it is not a dead end, for it leads to transformation in the Resurrection. Jesus shows us and leads the way.

As we reflect on the faces shown to us by our Three-in-One God, our entire faith and religious life may have to be reimagined. In this reimagining, we may find some healing for the inadequate and perhaps distorted images of God that we have carried around in our psyche. If we are angry at God, is it the Christian God or some poor substitute for this God that we once were taught? Perhaps our God has been a magical God who is supposed to make everything right. If we have not been able to relate to God in a personal and loving way, can we find a new incentive to do so in a different image of God? I know that many people have indeed begun to see and know God differently. And in that transformation of one's image of God comes a transformation of one's entire life.

Images of Humanity

Our Judeo-Christian biblical tradition tells us that human beings have been made in the image and likeness of God (Gen. 1:26). Therefore, our survey of the images of this God already tells us much about ourselves. And conversely, in looking at the images of humanity, we understand more about our God. The healthiest Christian tradition, rooted in the Bible and embraced by Celtic Christians, understands humanity, with all of God's creation, to be very good. Human beings are basically good by nature, though the same tradition is very aware of the power of sin and evil. I always thought that the goodness of humanity was self-evident. I am no longer certain that it is. I also see more clearly that our vision of people and things has a strong determining effect on how we deal with them. If we expect people to be good, we will treat them that way. We will be upset by injustices and not take them for granted. We will be moved to protect the goodness of all peoples. If we do not think people are basically good, we will easily excuse inhuman behavior.

A friend of mine teaches religious instruction to youngsters as part of his church's parish religious education program. On one occasion he asked his group of sixth graders, about eight of them, whether they thought human beings were basically good. They wrote their answers individually so as not to be influenced by each other. Only one in the group gave an affirmative answer to the query. The majority thought humanity to be basically bad. How will this affect their lives, beginning with the image of themselves?

Another anecdotal story came from Joseph J. Fahey, professor of religious studies at Manhattan College. He shared some thoughts with me after a talk I gave on Celtic Christianity and then sent me a journal with an article he had written on "Student Pessimism and Pelagian Optimism."[42] Fahey claims that thirty years of teaching Catholic college students has convinced him that they are basically anti-intellectual and pessimistic. Their comprehension of facts and skills without the corresponding willingness to reflect on matters is an indication of their anti-intellectualism. They simply parrot the things and opinions they have heard in the culture. The pessimism has to do with their expectations about war, violence, and the inequities of the capitalistic economic system. For instance, they understand the ways of violence and can describe countless ways to be violent, but they cannot name five ways to promote peace. They expect violence and war.

Fahey's thesis is that this proclivity to be pessimistic is deep in Western culture and is due to the prevalence of the teachings of Saint Augustine (354–430) about predestination, the significance and interpretation of original sin, and the toleration of just wars and the use of force to protect the truth. Fahey points to the Celtic theologian Pelagius (350–420) as having given us a different view of humanity with the expectations of the gospel for good, just, and peaceful behavior. Whether this antithesis is true or not does not take away from the observation of the pessimism that he finds in the young.

Recovering our Celtic sense of humanity means seeing the human being as good. Likewise, the present life and world is good. Human love and sexuality are gifts of God and not simply trials.[43] This is not a call to be naïve, for we must surely recognize the temptations to use God's gifts in a selfish and destructive manner. The cross is always present to the Celtic Christian vision, and we need help and protection against the powers of evil that seduce us to misuse our gifts. This does not, however, vitiate the goodness of the gifts themselves.

Community and the Common Good

A second aspect of the Celtic vision of humanity is a strong insistence on our connectedness to each other and to all creation. The Celts were, of course, a tribal people and this tribal nature influenced the early Christian church in Celtic countries. With no system of towns or cities, Ireland continued its tribal and clan way of living for many centuries. In Christian times, the monastery — actually a type of monastic village — and the monk were an important part of this tribal, community life. Monastic villages were communities, exhibiting a particular human pattern of living that embraced the spiritual, educational, economic, and political, all in one. Christianity brought some balance to the ancient tribal supremacy by introducing the value of each human person. In the second millennium, we have tended to lose the tribal, communal nature of our humanity, along with our connectedness to the earth and also our awareness of being feminine as well as masculine. We have become rugged individualists and have lost the sense of community and the demands of the common good.

A recovery of the sense that we are all intimately connected, that we all suffer and rejoice together in our human story, would help each of us and our world as well. This insight should certainly begin with Christian church groups. The "just God and me" spirituality, which prevails among many Christians as well as New Agers, is inadequate for facing modern life in general and fundamentally erroneous for living the Christian life. We are not alone, the Celts tell us. We are close to the angels, saints, and ancestors. We all are bound, one to another, in this present life. If any people on earth are poor, are oppressed, are denied their rights, then I am affected by their situation and part of me suffers the same things. The Christian view is that Christ is the head of us all. We all are his body. What one person experiences, good or bad, is experienced both by Christ the head and by all the members of the body. How profound were the words that Saul, the Pharisee persecuting Christians, heard on the road to Damascus, "Saul, Saul, why do you persecute me?" (Acts 9:4). Finally, we also know, from a biblical perspective, that our commonality, our unity in diversity, our oneness balancing our individuality are also a reflection of our being made in the image of the Three-in-One God whom we proclaim. The church, then, is our constant reminder to live in community, to share faith and vision and purpose, all based on keeping alive the memory of Jesus Christ and his gospel.

People of Place and People on Pilgrimage

A third image of humanity in Celtic Christianity comes from the valuing of place. It seems to me that ancient peoples, such as the Celts, had a much better grasp on who they were than do we moderns. In our times, we are constantly under pressure to find our identity in what we own and possess. "The one who dies with the most toys wins," says one cynical maxim of our age. Accumulate all you can and you will be important. How sad to see this right from infancy when parents shower a horde of toys and belongings on a child. What else, then, to expect from that time on, but that I am loved when I am given things?

The Celts understood themselves as belonging to a place, and specifically to the land, as well as belonging to their tribe, with its customs and expectations. Even in recent times, the Irish have been people of the land. There has been something very personal and intimate in how they have related to the land, respected it, and protected it. There is a need to belong to place, and the Celts knew it. The sense of unrootedness, of not really belonging, is pervasive in Western society today. Always on the move, we lose something in our self-understanding and self-love.

The spirituality of this tradition might help us all to value the earth in general and our own place in particular. My home, my garden, my place of existence is sacred space. But more than this, I believe that each of us needs to connect with the earth and its natural rhythms. Where can I go to find that spot which helps me to ground myself? Is it on top of a mountain or hill? Is it by the sea? Is it under a tree? It doesn't matter where, but it should be a place to which I can return and connect with myself on a deeper level, thus also connecting with my God.

Besides natural places, we also seem to need places and times in which we can return to a situation that enriches us and supports us in our faith journey. Instead of always looking for a new experience, it is helpful to return to a monastery, a retreat house, or a shrine that is a holy place for us. In such places we also come in contact with our souls in a way that is not always possible in the everyday hassle of our lives.

So, I suggest, if you are trying to deepen your spiritual life, you need to be rooted. You need to know where you belong. But ironically, you can take this with you. The paradox of place in the Celtic tradition is found in pilgrimage. We sometimes talk about the Irish as having wanderlust, a need to roam. I believe that the basis of this is in something much deeper. The Celtic monks were wanderers, but with a great purpose. They gave up all, even their own land, which they loved so much, as a way to follow Christ, who had no place to lay his head. Pilgrimage developed as a way to experience Christ, who emptied himself of everything for our sakes. I think pilgrimage can be a serious tool of the spiritual craft in our days too. It is a physical tool, requiring the complete person to be involved, body and soul. It is a communal tool, needing the help of others to travel. And, ideally, it means sharing with others along the way — sharing stories, sharing food, sharing faith. In America we don't have any religious sites of great significance for pilgrimages. Anything that we do have is rather recent. To go on pilgrimage to some of the old Celtic religious sites can be a truly uplifting experience. There we touch the faith of ages past — men and women of courage and vision, times of struggle and accomplishment. To stand on top of Skellig Michael off the coast of Kerry, to climb Croagh Patrick in Mayo, to walk to Glendalough in Wicklow — these are but the highlights of some thousands of possibilities in the Celtic countries.[44]

A Passionate People

The passionate warrior, a warrior with the soul of a poet, is another Celtic image of the human person that I like. Celtic spirituality is sometimes made out to be very romantic and totally consoling. The emphasis on the closeness to nature is, for instance, made to seem idyllic. But the truth lies elsewhere. Living in ancient Ireland, with no electricity or central heating, must not have been a comfortable existence for much of the year. A damp, cold, and dark climate prevails in the latitudes of the Celtic countries. Peoples there have been battling the elements and working hard for sustenance and protection for ages. In addition, these were warrior peoples. And Celtic Christianity absorbed the warrior spirit of its pagan ancestors. It was lived in a passionate and even fierce manner. Penance and asceticism were embraced as a way to follow Christ (and not as a way simply to punish sinful flesh). Being a Christian was a total way of life and not an adjunct to real life.

The monastic way of life, so central to Celtic Christianity, was an intense struggle with the powers of darkness. Monks saw their lives as a battle with the powers of evil, beginning with the demons that lay within their own souls. I don't think that we are any different from our ancestors. We too are attacked by demons, both within us and without us. We, however, tend to deny them or flee from them, while the monks took them on in battle. One conceptualization of this kind of battle came to me in a letter from a reader who explored some of this struggle with demons, especially as they become more apparent in midlife. This is part of Wayne's letter, in which he explored this feeling:

There is very little in life that I have "reason" to personally *feel* bad about. Yet, from time to time, I have visits from the dark side. I know why the psalmist asks for protection from "the terrors of the night." I once read a book titled "In the Jaws of the Black Dogs," a story of a lifelong battle with depression. I now think we are sometimes nipped in the heels by the black puppies!...Over the years I have come to see the black puppies as friends. They are reminders, in a Prozac/Viagra age, of the value of human experiences....I love the quote from Roberston Davies, "Turn the Wizard to the light, and you will see that he is also the Fool."

Bringing the dark side, the shadow, the black puppies, into the light is an important part of the spiritual life, often neglected in the desire to have only light. All spiritual traditions see the need to explore the dark and come to terms with it. The Celtic tradition speaks of the *anamchara*, or soul friend, as the one who helps us in this process and walks with us in our journey. It is another important reminder that we cannot make the spiritual journey alone.

A spiritual adventurer must set aside some time for prayer and solitude. Time may be taken for vigils and watching in the darkness. It may be climbing a mountain or standing in water with the arms outstretched in a crosslike fashion, or fasting and giving to the poor. These are some of the ways of spiritual combat of the Celtic tradition. Each of us has to find the right tools and battle instruments for today.

This kind of warrior energy, of self-discipline, of emptying oneself, is also the path of awareness of the needs of others. It brings together our own personal spiritual life with the call to do justice for all peoples, especially the poor and oppressed. The tools of spiritual warfare, of asceticism, are not practiced to turn in on oneself but to heighten one's awareness of the needs of others.

People of Prayer and Poetry

The last image of humanity from the Celtic tradition that I want to explore is that we are people of prayer and poetry. Perhaps this should be the most obvious characteristic. I leave it for last but do not want to presume it. There is no spiritual life without regular prayer. To pray always is the ideal. This doesn't mean one has to be reciting prayers all the time. It means to live in the presence of God and to do all with God and in God and through God. It means to be living the life of the Triune God, "in whom we live, and move, and have our being." It means little prayers, when we think of it, to lift up our hearts to that ever present God. Many prayers from the Celtic tradition show us how to do that. Here is a lovely prayer that was often recited upon rising:

> Bless to me, O God,
> Each thing mine eye sees;
> Bless to me, O God,
> Each sound mine ear hears;
> Bless to me, O God,
> Each odour that goes to my nostrils;
> Bless to me, O God,
> Each taste that goes to my lips;
> Each note that goes to my song,
> Each ray that guides my way,
> Each thing that I pursue,
> Each lure that tempts my will,
> The zeal that seeks my living soul,
> The Three that seek my heart,
> The zeal that seeks my living soul,
> The Three that seek my heart.[45]

And there must be special times of prayer as well. Perhaps the greatest treasure of valuable prayers for us today, as it was for ancient Christians, is the book of Psalms from the Hebrew Scriptures. The psalms are poetry. They are vivid and full of images. They express the passionate and intense and intimate engagement of the soul with God and with life. They make us look at reality and imagine things differently. It was the English Benedictine theologian Sebastian Moore who said that God is allowed to behave in the psalms as God is not allowed to behave in systematic theology! The psalms also express our feelings of trust and praise and thanks, as well as struggle, anger, and near despair. They engage all of us. The memorization of psalms was an important part of early Christian community life. With our small, printed manuals of books, we do not have to memorize them anymore, but they remain a wonderful resource in our instruments of the spiritual life. There is certainly great freedom in the way we do pray, but we are all called to be prayers and poets.

Images of the World

All we have said about God and humanity refers to our vision of the world. Little needs to be added but the reminder that recovering our Celtic roots may direct us to a different view of the world than our previous Christian teaching suggested. All of God's creation is good, and human beings, made in the divine image, are very good. The Catholic tradition, when true to itself, has a sacramental perception of the world. In other words, the Catholic view has been to apprehend the closeness of the divine in the very material realities of the world. Then it is only a simple step to celebrate this closeness of God in the material in the seven special epiphanies (called "sacraments") of this presence in the human rituals of baptism, confirmation, Eucharist, penance, anointing, marriage,

and holy orders. Unfortunately, this belief and sacramental worldview have not always been upheld. The world
has, at times and places, been looked upon as evil, something to get through. The human body has been seen as
a necessary evil too, especially in its sexual functions. Re-
gaining and affirming the goodness of all things is an
important part of anyone's spirituality and healing.

Modern science has helped us to see that all is truly one
and interrelated. Our bodies are the very substance of the
stars. We breathe the air that has circulated over the earth
for millions of years, the very air that Jesus and Mary and
the saints breathed. Within this oneness is a wonderful
diversity of species, of color and race. This diversity helps
to build up the oneness of the universe, which has come
from the hands of God.

The Celtic Christians were especially aware of the won-
ders of creation. Some of the greatest nature poetry has
come from the Irish medieval monks, who showed such
marvelous sensitivity to the song of a bird, the movement
of the wind, the light of sun or moon coming through
trees. Some of the most wonderful stories of these monks
and Christians tell us of a view of reality in which animals
and humans were friends and co-creatures, all together
praising God as they helped each other.

The Christian call is to care for the earth and see it as
holy, to reverence it and help it to bear fruit, fruit that can
be shared with all. With their communal sensitivity, the
Celts knew that all this must be shared. Today, Christians
who are well-off need to look at their own lifestyles, their
own consumption of the earth's goods, and see how this
affects all other peoples, particularly those who have less.

All Is Brought Together in Christ

God, humanity, and all creation are brought together in
Jesus the Christ. The Christ embodies who God is for us.

The Christ shows us what humanity is supposed to be. The incarnation, God in flesh, manifests the goodness of the material world. And it is the Catholic tradition in particular, with its sacramental consciousness, that has seen this Christ to be alive in the church, in the sacraments, in the community of believers. It is Christ who calls us together to be one, to overcome our differences, to forgive each other, to accept reconciliation with God and with each other. It is the Christ who shares the Spirit with us, the Spirit who moves and lives throughout all our being.

Our Celtic roots, then, ultimately take us back, as Christian disciples, to Christ, the great hero. They root us in the mystical body of Christ, the Christian community. They help us, through Christ, to find each other. They help us to live, through our imagination and memory and faith, lives that are already aware of the close presence of our God, of the saints, and of all our ancestors. Irish Catholics might find in these Celtic roots the healing and reconciliation to live fuller and happier lives. I pray that you who read these pages, like many who have read and listened before you, find them nurturing for your faith. May Patrick, Bridget, Columcille, and all the saints accompany you in this journey of faith, along with all those alive today who similarly seek the face of the living God. I call upon the Triune God to guide you on your path of healing, of reconciliation, and to the wholeness that God desires for you.

> The eye of the great God be upon you,
> The eye of the God of glory be on you,
> The eye of the Son of Mary Virgin be on you,
> The eye of the Spirit mild be on you,
> To aid you and to shepherd you;
> Oh the kindly eye of the Three be on you,
> To aid you and to shepherd you.[46]

Epilogue

A Celtic Dream and Hope

*L*IKE MARTIN LUTHER KING, I have a dream, a vision and a hope for a better world. As we move into the third millennium, I dream that we will let go of many of the divisions, fears, and antagonisms that marked the second millennium. The image of our world, seen now as a fragile orb in outer space, will prompt us to be more aware of the unity of the human race and how we are responsible to each other, to our children, and to our God for the future of our planet. I envision a world that knows we are all brothers and sisters and that we are people who care for each other, especially the most needy. We will all be secure in our particular identities of nationality, gender, race, and religion. We will not need to put others down or control others for our own self-aggrandizement. The unity of our human family will truly be enriched by the diversity of the many human groupings.

I further dream and hope that the Irish Catholic community would be particularly adventurous in building this new world. As a people who have suffered, who have been oppressed and marginalized, rejected and scarred, as a people who have worked hard to find meaning for themselves and their children, I hope they would bring special gifts to this human enterprise.

The Irish arriving in the New World experienced themselves as aliens and not welcomed. Through hard work, faith, and courage they built a strong church to help them through the difficult times of transition and adjustment. They rose to positions of responsibility in politics and public service. Eventually they did well in the economic and business world, and in the academic world as well. They have finally arrived. With this arrival and acceptance comes the great critical moment. Will success and achievement dull them to their previous history and the possibility of relating it to contemporary problems? Or can they draw on their story to contribute to the ongoing story? No doubt, so far, the Irish have done some of both.

It is significant that the Irish American community has been important to those who have been working to heal and reconcile the divided Irish in Northern Ireland. Previously, many Irish Americans have contributed to the ongoing violence by supporting the IRA and keeping the hatred and antagonism alive. In more recent times, the efforts of Senator George Mitchell, as well as many others, have brought about constructive efforts to heal the breach, a divide that is no doubt deep and built upon centuries of ill will.

I hope that this same reconciling effort would engage Irish Catholics on many other levels and in many other arenas. The Irish have come from a longstanding Celtic love of the land and closeness to the forces of God's good creation. It is good to see them actively involved in ecological concerns and in helping human beings to heal the estrangement that they have with the earth.

As described earlier, the Irish experience has many parallels with the black community and also with the Native American experience. May they remember the similarity of their backgrounds and learn to be open to and understanding of them, the Jews, and such ethnic and national groups who still have not been absorbed into the American scene as the Irish have. A particular challenge for the future will be the welcoming of new groups into our pluralistic society. Asians are becoming more a part of the American fabric, and they bring new gifts. In the future, Hispanics will be a very large part of the people of the Catholic Church. Their gifts, their talents and abilities, will contribute to the future church, just as the gifts of the Irish once did. Will the Irish, as well as other ethnic groups, be big enough and open enough to want to learn from them and share with them? I pray that this will be so.

The Irish, heirs of a Celtic Church that felt itself so close to the East and to that great mystical tradition, can also help us to move into a future where we heal the great division of East and West, Catholic and Orthodox, and also to be open to other religions of the East, with their mystical and contemplative traditions.

Heirs of a church tradition that also treasured gifts of both men and women, the Irish Catholic community also might help reconcile men and women in society and in the church. Surely we are going through a difficult period, a transition period in our understanding of male and female roles. Openness must replace fear. Acceptance and tolerance must replace any demeaning attitudes and defensive use of ridicule.

There are so many areas that are in need of healing and reconciliation. My perspective in this book has been to begin with personal healing and reconciliation. By accepting ourselves, our history and our present situation, we may be able to contribute to the healing and reconciliation of a church, a society, a world, and a universe that beg for such healing. At least we can begin with this vision and let it influence our way of living. At least I hope that can be so. I dream of such a possibility.

Appendix

Some Ways to Reclaim One's Celtic Roots

ELTIC CHRISTIANITY refers to the particular ways that the universal Christian church was inculturated in the Celtic countries, principally from the fifth through the twelfth centuries. There is no such thing as a Celtic Christian church today, nor do I wish, in any way, to advocate a kind of Celtic "sect." Nevertheless, perspectives and view-points from the Celtic Christian tradition might be of help in leading a Christian life today. I offer the following suggestions for the reader who is looking for a richer spiritual life. Choose one or more with which to begin and add others as you are able. They are merely suggestions. Names of books or authors mentioned can be found in the bibliography.

1. For a new, poetic, down-to-earth manner of praying, start reading selections from the *Carmina Gadelica*. The writings of Esther deWaal can also be helpful in introducing these prayers to you. While you are at it, reeducate and stimulate your religious imagination by paying attention to good religious art, music, and literature. Much of traditional Celtic music, in particular, can open up your mystical side. Being spiritual doesn't mean being dull, boring, or in poor taste.

2. Now turn to the meat of the sacred Scriptures. If these are not familiar to you, read the Gospels for a while. Come to know Christ as your friend, who lives with you

and suffers and rejoices with you; but come to know him also as your hero. And then start praying the psalms. Look in one of the Celtic books, at images, for example, from the Book of Kells, and see the great devotion that the Celtic monks had for the Scriptures. Find a type of daily prayer that combines Scripture and modern forms of prayer (see Fitzgerald and Rupp).

3. Read some of the lives of the saints. There are some good books on the Celtic saints (see Sellner, Earle and Maddox, Woods) that will introduce you to the Celtic world and help you to pray with the Celtic saints as well. You might want to go to primary sources and read, for example, the wonderful *Confession of Saint Patrick,* as well as other early writings of the Celtic church. Let these saints become your friends and fellow pilgrims in life. Gradually, start to read other books and periodicals on matters of faith, good Christian living, and spirituality.

4. Go on a pilgrimage (not just a tour!) of Ireland and other Celtic countries. There are various pilgrimage groups available now. Touch and feel the ancient holy sites and also feel how the spirit is still alive. Take the children with you. If you skip Disneyland, you'll have the funds to do it, and you'll also provide a more authentic and enjoyable experience (see Pemberton).

5. If you are not ready for a pilgrimage, or want to know more after making one, attend a workshop or retreat on Celtic spirituality. These are available on both a daylong and weekend-long basis (write to *Anamchairde* for listings). Go to a monastery or retreat house regularly for an hour, a day, or a weekend to find a place where you belong and know that you have the support of others in your spiritual journey.

6. Find a favorite place in nature in which to slow down and feel at one with God and the cosmos. Return to it often and spend some time in solitude, silence, and stillness without a radio or Walkman. Recover the nat-

ural sense of wonder and awe that you had as a child. Slow down your life and do not be afraid of what goes on inside you. Let it emerge and reflect upon it.

7. Now begin to share what goes on within your heart and soul with an *anamchara* (soul friend). This person can be a confessor, a spiritual director, or a friend with whom you have a mutual and open relationship of sharing in a totally honest way.

8. If possible, find a small group that shares your ideals and goals. Pray with each other; share with each other. Covenant with each other to do some spiritual practices, or even countercultural practices, for example, to observe the Sunday Sabbath for rest and prayer.

9. Do not, however, let your small support group become a sect or a clique. Take part in your parish and touch the wider, universal church that is the body of Christ. Nourish your spiritual life with the sacraments, especially Sunday Mass, regular Holy Communion, and occasional celebration of the sacrament of reconciliation (see Upton).

10. True spirituality always brings an increase of compassion to one's life. It cannot just be a "God and me" feel-good situation. Celtic spirituality was honed by people living on the margins, a people often in suffering and pain. Remember your ancestors and reach out to the needs of others. Social justice is an essential ingredient of the spiritual life.

11. Don't forget that the Celtic saints were usually great ascetics. You don't have to imitate their standing in cold water to pray, but the example is a reminder of the need for discipline in our lives. Nothing can be done without the DDTs: discipline, determination, and time. While practices such as fasting and keeping solitary vigil at night still have value, the modern asceticism may be to take the time out of a busy day to be silent for twenty minutes, to meditate and thereby forgo something else, like television. Simplicity of lifestyle also is a modern as-

ceticism worthy of consideration. A frugality in the use of the earth's bounty is also a contribution to honoring creation.

12. Be attentive and open to the need, as well as the opportunities, for forgiveness, healing, and reconciliation in your daily life. Become, by your manner of living, a "minister of reconciliation" for a scarred and aching world.

Notes

Introduction

1. Timothy Joyce, *Celtic Christianity: A Sacred Tradition, A Vision of Hope* (Maryknoll, N.Y.: Orbis, 1998).

2. Timothy Joyce, *A Retreat with Patrick: Discovering God in All* (Cincinnati: Saint Anthony Messenger Press, 2000).

1. American Catholics and Their Journey

3. "The Irish Famine and American Catholic Spirituality," *Anamchairde* 3, no. 3 (summer 1997), 1ff. *Anamchairde* is the quarterly newsletter of the Anamchairde Network (Cincinnati).

4. Such as *Blackrobe, Catholics, The Lonely Passion of Judith Hearne, The Colour of Blood,* and *The Statement.*

5. I was in Rome when the Dalai Lama visited and stayed with our Benedictine community there. He had a large following of Westerners, mostly Catholics, eager to hear him. It was instructive to hear him counsel such followers to go back to their own tradition and find their spiritual roots there.

6. John Cassian (360–435) brought Eastern monasticism to France and the West. His writings include the *Institutes* and *Conferences.*

7. Saint Benedict (480–547), of Nursia, Italy, wrote his Rule as a compendium of the monastic tradition. He is known as the Patriarch of Western Monasticism.

8. See, for instance, the works of Esther deWaal, Norvene Vest, and Kathleen Norris.

2. The Faith of Our Irish Ancestors

9. For a recent and well-documented treatment of the place of this extraordinary churchman, see John Cooney, *John*

Charles McQuaid: Ruler of Catholic Ireland (Dublin: O'Brien Press, 1999). Though McQuaid was an intensely guarded and private man, he kept copious notes and documentation that are all accessible today.

10. John J. Ó Ríordáin, *Irish Catholic Spirituality, Celtic and Roman* (Dublin: Columba Press, 1998).

11. Ibid., 134–35.

12. One early pioneer was Canon Pádraig Ó Fiannachta, who, as Dean of Celtic Studies at the Seminary of Maynooth, was often ridiculed for his interests. In retirement he has opened the *Díseart*, a Celtic educational and cultural institute in Dingle Town, County Kerry.

13. See Seán Mac Réamoinn, "With the Past, in the Present, for the Future," in *Religion in Ireland: Past, Present and Future,* ed. Denis Carroll (Dublin: Columba Press, 1999), 121.

14. See, for instance, Kieran McKeown and Hugh Arthurs, eds., *Soul Searching: Personal Stories of the Search for Meaning in Modern Ireland* (Dublin: Columba Press, 1997), and Tony Flannery, *From the Inside: A Priest's View of the Catholic Church* (Dublin: Mercier Press, 1999).

15. I refer to the fine ministries of Fathers Michael Rodgers and Marcus Losack at Glendalough; Canon Pádraig "Ó Fiannachta" in Dingle; Father Frank Fahey at Balintubber Abbey in Mayo; and Sister Mary Minehan in Kildare. Further references can be found in Joyce, *Celtic Christianity*.

16. Colm Kilcoyne, "The Present Crisis: A Way Forward?" in Carroll, ed., *Religion in Ireland*, 156–57.

3. Irish American Catholicism

17. The data and statistics for this section have been taken from Charles R. Morris, *American Catholic* (New York: Random House, 1997).

18. On the Canadian scene, Grosse Point in Quebec was a landing place for Irish immigrants and the scene of numerous deaths due to diseases carried by the travelers or soon contracted locally.

19. By the 1880s, 80 percent of the Irish lived in cities, compared to 20 percent for other Americans.

20. One factor that marks the Irish immigrants as different from later groups is the large number of women who immigrated, often on their own. In other groups, the men came first and sent for women only when they were settled.

21. Terry Golway, *The Irish in America*, ed. Michael Coffey (New York: Hyperion, 1997), 47. See chapter 2, "The Parish, The Building of a Community," 45–93.

22. Morris, *American Catholic*, 111.

23. I have treated this subject in some detail in my book *Celtic Christianity: A Sacred Tradition, A Vision of Hope*. See particularly chapter 6. In that book, I was indebted to the studies of the Irish American in therapy as documented by Monica McGoldrick in her fine book *Ethnicity and Family Therapy* (New York: Guildford Press, 1982).

24. Michael Patrick McDonald, in his book *All Souls: A Family Story from Southie* (Boston: Beacon Press, 1999), has written a very insightful and poignant picture of growing up in Southie and developments there over the past thirty years.

25. The matter is reviewed by Mark S. Massa, in *Catholics and American Culture* (New York: Crossroad, 1999), 1–3.

26. The irony is even more striking when we remember that the Irish were often looked down upon in Europe in the same derogatory way that the blacks were in America.

4. From Certainty to Confusion

27. The data and fuller description of the social changes involved can be found in writings such as Jay Dolan, *American Catholic Experience: A History from Colonial Times to the Present* (Garden City, N.Y.: Doubleday, 1985); Andrew Greeley, *The Church and the Suburbs* (New York: Sheed and Ward, 1959); Morris, *American Catholic*.

28. The affectionate nickname "Uncle Fultie" was bestowed on him as a worthy rival in popularity to "Uncle Miltie," Milton Berle, who at that time starred in the most watched program on television, *The Milton Berle Show*.

29. "Gaudium et Spes: Pastoral Constitution on the Church in the Modern World," *Vatican Council II*, trans. and ed. Austin Flannery, O.P. (Dublin: Dominican Publications, 1996), no. 1.

5. Choosing the Path to Healing

30. For the following reflections on healing I am much inspired by the thoughts of Father William A. Meninger, *The Process of Forgiveness* (New York: Continuum, 1999).

31. Blue Cloud Abbey was founded in 1950 as a center for the missionary monks already serving the Native Americans on local reservations. Though its formal patroness is Our Lady of the Snows, the abbey is named after Blue Cloud, a Sioux chief.

32. This center was founded by Father Neal Carlin, a priest of the Diocese of Derry. It is situated at 11 Queen Street in Derry. The House also runs Saint Anthony's Retreat Centre in Dundrean, County Donegal. A Presbyterian minister and a Church of England priest now also participate in this ministry.

33. It is gratifying to see attempts in Ireland to deal with such issues openly and in the pursuit of healing. Bishop Laurence Ryan, of Kildare and Leighlin, writes movingly in his foreword to a book edited by Father Frank Fahey, *In Need of Healing: If Anyone Is Listening* (Dublin: Veritas Publications, 1999). Conversations about unmarried mothers, the authoritarian church, sex abuses, and so forth are delicately and sensitively examined in first-person accounts.

6. Finding One's Celtic Spiritual Roots (1): Imagination and Story

34. John Hopkins, "Things Celtic," 1998. John is a teacher, a father of two children, and helps run the "James Joyce Ramble" every year in Boston.

35. Though I had long suspected the Celtic-Jewish connection, I am indebted for the deeper comprehension of this insight to a talk given by Jane Redmont and reflected in her book *When In Doubt, Sing: Prayer in Daily Life* (New York: HarperCollins, 1999).

36. See Thomas Moore, *Care of the Soul* (New York: Harper and Row, 1992).

37. The usual term for this is "magician," but our common understanding of this word doesn't correspond to this image of the searcher for reality in the cosmos.

7. Finding One's Celtic Spiritual Roots (2): Images of God, Humanity, and the Universe

38. Paula Murphy, writing from Sligo, Ireland, May 1996. See also her poem based on the biblical *Song of Songs* in Joyce, *Celtic Christianity*, 138.

39. "I Lie Down This Night," in Alexander Carmichael, *Carmina Gadelica: Hymns and Incantations* (Hudson, N.Y.: Lindisfarne Books, 1994), no. 327, p. 299.

40. In writing about God as Father and Son, I am quite aware that these images are difficult for some people, whether because of their poor experiences of fatherhood, the unfortunate identification of fatherhood with patriarchy, or their emerging feminine consciousness. I agree that more diverse images of God are needed and that some of them, like mother and wisdom, should portray a feminine side of God. But I am not ready to completely jettison the traditional images of Father, Son, and Spirit. The substitution of images such as Creator-Redeemer-Sanctifier lack the relational and personal element, since they are functional images and are really attributable to all three persons. We seem to need reconciliation with "father" in our own culture today, and God the Father is an important help for us, as this God is Other and yet takes on intimate and even paternal, as well as maternal, characteristics. There is also the reality of Christ being a historical figure into whose body and life we are initiated at baptism and whose relationship with God we are to imitate. I hope my emphasis on the mystery and transcendence of the first person of the Trinity is understood as my main point here. Our principal name or metaphor for this person has been Father.

41. The Sequence is a hymn that is sung following the second Scripture reading on Pentecost Sunday. It is a twelfth-century composition. See the Roman Missal.

42. Joseph J. Fahey, "Student Pessimism and Pelagian Optimism," *Listening, Journal of Religion and Culture* 31, no. 1 (winter 1996): 37–54.

43. See J. Philip Newell's reflections in *Listening to the Heartbeat of God* (New York: Paulist Press, 1997), especially chapter 1, "Listening to the Goodness: Pelagius," 8–22.

44. For a wonderful reflection on the nature of pilgrimage

as well as the description of notable pilgrimage sites in Ireland, Scotland, Wales, and the Isle of Man, I highly recommend Cintra Pemberton, *Soulfaring: Celtic Pilgrimage Then and Now* (Harrisburg, Pa.: Morehouse, 1999). Some of these sites are also described in Joyce, *Celtic Christianity.*

45. *Carmina Gadelica*, no. 226, p. 199.

46. Ibid., no. 277, p. 252.

Annotated Bibliography

Anamchairde, a quarterly newsletter with articles, book reviews, and listings of events in Celtic spirituality. Anamchairde Network, 2374 Madison Rd., Cincinnati, OH 45208, or www.anamchairde.org.

Carmichael, Alexander. *Carmina Gadelica: Hymns and Incantations.* Hudson, N.Y.: Lindisfarne Books, 1994. Excerpts also available in smaller editions. A wonderful collection of prayers collected in the Scottish highlands and islands in the nineteenth century.

Carroll, Denis, ed. *Religion in Ireland: Past, Present and Future.* Dublin: Columba Press, 1999. A series of essays on the Roman Catholic Church, the church of Ireland, Presbyterians, Jews, minority voices, and other related topics looking at religion in Ireland, with some hopeful views for its future.

Clancy, Padraigin. *Celtic Threads: Exploring the Wisdom of Our Heritage.* Dublin: Veritas Publications, 1999. A number of essays looking at the Celtic spiritual roots in Ireland by authors such as John J. Ó Ríordáin, Diarmuid Ó Laoghaire, and others. Since most of the books on Celtic Christianity to be published so far have largely come from Great Britain, and to a lesser degree from America, this is a significant contribution by Irish authors.

Coffey, Michael, ed., text by Terry Golway, with many other contributors. *The Irish in America.* New York: Hyperion, 1997. A book of essays, poems, and photographs portraying the Irish famine and the Irish American experience of parish, precinct, and politics.

Davies, Oliver, and Fiona Bowie, eds. *Celtic Christian Spirituality: An Anthology of Medieval and Modern Sources.* New York: Continuum, 1995. The finest one-volume collection of medieval poetry and prose, the oral tradition of Ireland and Scotland, plus modern poetry. It also has an excellent introduction to Celtic spirituality.

Davies, Oliver, trans. with the collaboration of Thomas O'Loughlin. *Celtic Spirituality*. The Classics of Western Spirituality Series. New York: Paulist Press, 1999. This is the finest compendium in the English language of primary texts of Celtic Spirituality.

DeWaal, Esther. *Every Earthly Blessing: Rediscovering the Celtic Tradition*. New edition. Harrisburg, Pa.: Morehouse, 1999. A very helpful guide through the prayers of the *Carmina Gadelica* to the beauty of the Celtic vision.

———. *The Celtic Way of Prayer: The Recovery of the Religious Imagination*. New York: Doubleday, 1997. More help from deWaal in using the Celtic tradition to pray better.

Earle, Mary, and Sylvia Maddox. *Praying with the Celtic Saints*. Winona, Wis.: Saint Mary's Press, 1999. Getting to know some of the Celtic saints and, with them, finding a down-to-earth way to pray.

Fahey, Frank. *In Need of Healing: If Anyone Is Listening*. Dublin: Veritas Publications, 1999. A series of first-person accounts centered on seven topics of areas of Irish church life in need of healing and reconciliation.

Fitzgerald, William John, and Joyce Rupp. *A Contemporary Celtic Prayer Book*. Chicago: ACTA Publications, 1998. This is the finest small book of prayer available that gives short daily morning and evening prayers as well as prayers for special occasions, all in the Christian prayer tradition using Celtic imaginative prayers and reflections.

Flannery, Tony. *From the Inside: A Priest's View of the Catholic Church*. Dublin: Mercier Press, 1999. A critical but loving view of the Irish church today. This Irish Redemptorist priest helps to articulate the questions that many Catholics ask.

Jones, John Miriam. *With an Eagle's Eye: A Seven-Day Sojourn in Celtic Spirituality*. Notre Dame, Ind.: Ave Maria Press, 1996. Seven sets of reflections on various themes of Celtic spirituality, useful for a retreat or daily prayer times.

Joyce, Timothy J. *Celtic Christianity: A Sacred Tradition, A Vision of Hope.* Maryknoll, N.Y.: Orbis Books, 1998. A historical and theological look at the Celtic Christian experience and what it offers Christians today.

————. *A Retreat with Patrick: Discovering God in All.* Cincinnati: Saint Anthony Messenger Press, 2000. Seven daily reflections on themes of Celtic spirituality based on the writings of Saint Patrick.

McKeown, Kieran, and Hugh Arthurs, eds. *Soul Searching: Personal Stories of the Search for Meaning in Modern Ireland.* Dublin: Columba Press, 1997. Short and very personal stories of various men and women, from different religious traditions, sharing their spiritual search in the context of modern Ireland.

Maguire, Mairead Corrigan. *The Vision of Peace: Faith and Hope in Northern Ireland.* Maryknoll, N.Y.: Orbis Books, 1999. Writings by a Nobel Peace Prize winner on the subject of reconciliation, healing, and forgiveness among the people of Northern Ireland.

Meninger, William. *The Process of Forgiveness.* New York: Continuum, 1999. A very inspiring book, with helpful exercises and mediations to aid in the process of forgiveness.

Morris, Charles R. *American Catholic.* New York: Random House, 1997. Very readable description of the story of Catholicism in America. The nineteenth-century beginnings, as here related, are a large help to understanding how much the Irish church influenced and formed the entire American scene.

Newell, J. Philip. *Listening to the Heartbeat of God: A Celtic Spirituality.* New York: Paulist Press, 1997. Reflections on the goodness of creation, the imagination, and other Celtic themes.

————. *One Foot in Eden: A Celtic View of the Stages of Life.* New York: Paulist Press, 1999. Reflections from the Celtic tradition as applied to the seven stages of human growth — from birth to death.

O'Carroll, Noreen. *Virginia's Questions: Why I Am Still a Catholic.* Dublin: Columba Press, 1998. An Irish woman shares her criticism of the Catholic Church, and also her reasons for hanging in.

O'Donoghue, Noel Dermot. *The Mountain behind the Mountain: Aspects of the Celtic Tradition.* Edinburgh: T. & T. Clark, 1993. This book is a real gem and will appeal to anyone seeking a more theological view of the Celtic tradition, including its association with the vision of Pierre Teilhard de Chardin.

Ó Ríordáin, John J. *Irish Catholic Spirituality, Celtic and Roman.* Dublin: Columba Press, 1998. An excellent synopsis of the history of the Irish church as being both Celtic and Roman. Its final chapter, on the state of the church today, is insightful and challenging.

————. *The Music of What Happens: A Celtic Spirituality from the Inside.* Dublin: Columba Press, 1996. A view of various Irish spiritual persons and practices and how the old Celtic vision has lived on in the modern Irish church.

Pemberton, Cintra. *Soulfaring: Celtic Pilgrimage Then and Now.* Harrisburg, Pa.: Morehouse, 1999. This book has an excellent introduction to explain the historical and spiritual meaning of pilgrimage. It then describes, meditatively, various pilgrim sites in the Celtic countries.

Sellner, Edward C. *Wisdom of the Celtic Saints.* Notre Dame, Ind.: Ave Maria Press, 1993. A thirty-two page, excellent introduction to the Celtic church and Celtic spirituality is followed by delightful stories and sayings from nineteen Celtic saints.

Upton, Julia. *A Time for Embracing: Reclaiming Reconciliation.* Collegeville, Minn.: Liturgical Press, 1999. A look at reconciliation in American society, in the Bible, and the sacrament of reconciliation both in history and today.

Woods, Richard J. *The Spirituality of the Celtic Saints.* Maryknoll, N.Y.: Orbis Books, 2000. This is probably the most thorough overview of the Celtic saints, their lives and their significance. It treats themes such as social justice, the status of women, and the concern for the natural environment.

Also by

Timothy Joyce

Celtic Christianity
A Sacred Tradition, A Vision of Hope
ISBN 1-57075-176-5

As Timothy Joyce shows, Celtic spirituality appeals
to mind, body, and spirit. Joyous and mystical,
it affirms the goodness of creation and the gifts
of women; it blossoms in poetry, myth, and song.
Celtic Christianity offers a rediscovery of an ancient
tradition that can sustain spiritual seekers and
renew the church today.

Of Related Interest

The Spirituality of the Celtic Saints
Richard J. Woods
ISBN 1-57075-316-4

"This new book avoids the wooly sentimentality
so often attached to work on Celtic spirituality.
Woods shows that Ireland is, in fact, what we
proverbially say: It is the land of saints
and scholars."
— *Lawrence S. Cunningham*

Please support your local bookstore, or call 1-800-258-5838

For a free catalog, please write us at
Orbis Books, Box 308
Maryknoll, NY 10545-0308
or visit our website at www.maryknoll.org/orbis

Thank you for reading *Celtic Quest*.
We hope you enjoyed it.